You Sound Just Like...

ALSO BY SHEREE HOMER
AND FROM MCFARLAND

Under the Influence of Classic Country: Profiles of 36 Performers of the 1940s to Today (2019)

Dig That Beat!: Interviews with Musicians at the Root of Rock 'n' Roll (2015)

Rick Nelson, Rock 'n' Roll Pioneer (2012)

Catch That Rockabilly Fever: Personal Stories of Life on the Road and in the Studio (2010)

You Sound Just Like...

Behind the Scenes with 40 Musical Tribute Artists

SHEREE HOMER

Foreword by James L. Neibaur

McFarland & Company, Inc., Publishers
Jefferson, North Carolina

LIBRARY OF CONGRESS CATALOGUING-IN-PUBLICATION DATA

Names: Homer, Sheree, 1978– author. | Neibaur, James L., 1958– writer of foreword.
Title: You sound just like... : behind the scenes with 40 musical tribute artists / Sheree Homer ; foreword by James L. Neibaur.
Description: Jefferson, North Carolina : McFarland & Company, Inc., Publishers, 2023. | Includes bibliographical references and index.
Identifiers: LCCN 2022052070 | ISBN 9781476681658 (paperback : acid free paper) ∞
ISBN 9781476647388 (ebook)
Subjects: LCSH: Celebrity impersonators—Biography. | Celebrity impersonators—Interviews. | Elvis Presley impersonators—Biography. | Elvis Presley impersonators—Interviews. | Musicians—Biography. | Musicians—Interviews. | BISAC: MUSIC / History & Criticism
Classification: LCC ML394 .H667 2023 | DDC 782.42164092/2 [B]—dc23/eng/20221101
LC record available at https://lccn.loc.gov/2022052070

BRITISH LIBRARY CATALOGUING DATA ARE AVAILABLE

ISBN (print) 978-1-4766-8165-8
ISBN (ebook) 978-1-4766-4738-8

© 2023 Sheree Homer. All rights reserved

No part of this book may be reproduced or transmitted in any form or by any means, electronic or mechanical, including photocopying or recording, or by any information storage and retrieval system, without permission in writing from the publisher.

On the cover: *clockwise from top left* Julie Myers as Stevie Nicks (courtesy Julie Myers); Lisa Irion in a publicity photo for her tribute to Cher (courtesy Lisa Irion); Caden Gamblin's tribute to the King of Rock and Roll (courtesy Caden Gamblin); Johnny Rogers as Buddy Holly (courtesy Johnny Rogers); Tammi Savoy paid special tribute to Ruth Brown in a set at the U.K.'s Rhythm Riot (courtesy Tammi Savoy); microphone © Billion Photos/Shutterstock

Printed in the United States of America

McFarland & Company, Inc., Publishers
Box 611, Jefferson, North Carolina 28640
www.mcfarlandpub.com

For all the tribute artists and their fans,
thanks for keeping the music alive!

Acknowledgments

Without God, this project would not have been possible. Words cannot begin to thank Him enough for introducing me to the wonderfully talented, generous and kind folks whom I have met in the music community and for blessing me with both the talent and the opportunity to tell their stories. Music has always been my sanctuary. Listening to it and writing about it give me inner peace and solace when the world around me gets too crazy. Music is as essential to me as breathing.

Many thanks, as always, to my mom, who introduced me to rock and roll and for being the best mom anyone could ever hope for. Your unconditional love and support have always encouraged me to pursue my dreams. I cherish all the happy memories of us attending concerts together. I also thank you for editing my pages.

Thanks, too, to my brother Gary, who has helped my mom and me through several rough patches. We wouldn't have survived without you. You came to the rescue when we needed you most.

Extra special thanks to all the tribute artists for providing my book with photos and invaluable insight into your lives and careers. It is an honor to tell others about your talents.

I am grateful to the individuals who helped me gather contact information and research materials, set up interviews, and obtain photos, in particular Kelly Hali Chelette, Jennifer Hughes, Dick McVey and Tcheania Watkins.

Table of Contents

Acknowledgments — vi
Foreword by James L. Neibaur — 1
Preface — 3

One: The Rockabilly Hepcat: Elvis Presley — 5
    Kavan Hashemian 5 • Travis LeDoyt 8 • Caden Gamblin 12 • Ricky Aron 14 • Jake Slater 16 • Finley Watkins 18

Two: "Rave On" for Me: Buddy Holly — 21
    Johnny Rogers 21 • John Mueller 23

Three: "It'll Be Me": Jerry Lee Lewis — 29
    Luke Stroud 29 • Jared Freiburg 32 • Doug Cooke 37 • Jacob Tolliver 41

Four: Pop–Rock and Roll Icons — 46
    Al Jackson (Fats Domino) 46 • Jesse Aron (Roy Orbison) 51 • Rick Lindy (Roy Orbison) 53 • Garry Moore (Little Richard) 57 • David Bogle (Ricky Nelson) 59 • Scott Hinds (Carl Perkins) 63 • Ty Stone (James Brown) 67 • Pete Hutton (Ral Donner) 70

Five: Women Who Rock — 73
    Tammi Savoy (Diana Ross) 73 • Julie Myers (Stevie Nicks) 77 • Laura West (Ann-Margret) 79 • Lisa Irion (Cher) 81 • Amberley Beatty (Patsy Cline) 85 • Elaine Wesley (Patsy Cline) 88

Six: "Hello, I'm Johnny Cash" — 91
    Zach McNabb 91 • Pete Storm 94 • Christopher Essex 97

Seven: "Walk a Mile in My Shoes": 1970s Elvis — 100
    Leo Days 100 • Doug Church 104 • Michael St. Angel 108 •

Table of Contents

Gib Maynard 110 • Bill Cherry 113 • Ted Torres Martin 116 • Johnny Thompson 120 • Dwight Icenhower 125 • John Lyons 128 • Garry Wesley 132 • Jay Dupuis 136

Chapter Notes   143
Bibliography   147
Index   149

Foreword

By James L. Neibaur

Many of us with an interest in rock and roll's rich history feel short-changed by the fact that we were born too late to have experienced live performances by the genre's pioneers. Creating a veritable cultural revolution as far back as the mid–1950s, performers Elvis Presley, Fats Domino, Chuck Berry, Buddy Holly, Little Richard, Jerry Lee Lewis, Carl Perkins, etc., were not only creating a new sound, they were themselves learning how to expand it into the most comprehensive music of the 20th century.

Tribute artists who perform in the way and manner of these classic stars work hard to fill the gap for those of us who didn't get to experience the originals. Their hard work, dedication and celebration of the performers and their music bring a new appreciation to subsequent generations, helping them to realize the importance of the music's history and the men and women responsible for its foundation.

Sheree Homer is a popular music historian who has provided indispensable studies of rockabilly, country music, Rick Nelson and other subjects. She is also too young to have experienced the vintage stars. Exploring the many different tribute artists over the years, Ms. Homer decided to write a book about them. Not content with merely dispensing her own opinion and experiences as a member of the audience, she has conducted interviews with the forty tribute artists chosen for this book, allowing us to understand each one's approach.

There are many tributes to Elvis Presley, whom some believe is the single most important figure in the history of popular music. Unlike some of his 1950s contemporaries, Elvis didn't fizzle out as styles and concepts changed. Persevering with movie soundtracks when The Beatles and other British rock groups took over the music charts, Elvis emerged with perhaps the best performance of his career with a 1968 TV special that reminded everyone he was still King. The tribute artists

Foreword

who salute him choose different aspects of his long career, from the early chart-topper whose Sun Studio roots led to an RCA contract and hits that define the rock and roll genre. Then there is Elvis of the middle years, culminating with the 1968 special, and finally, there is the sequined superstar, the legend, who spent his remaining years still occupying the highest mountain top. In Buddy Holly's short career, ending tragically with a 1959 plane crash, he laid down tracks that continue to have a towering influence. Johnny Cash extended the parameters of country music into the popular mainstream. Each of these important performers is represented by heartfelt tributes.

But Sheree Homer's book does not limit itself to the pioneers. Realizing that tribute artists cover the entire spectrum of popular music, she also spotlights performers who offer tributes to the likes of Cher, Stevie Nicks, Ann-Margret and Diana Ross.

It is difficult not to be impressed by these performers. Imagine having the ability to recapture the distinct voice of Elvis, Johnny Cash, Roy Orbison or Patsy Cline. Think of the hard work involved in conveying the powerful stage presence of Jerry Lee Lewis, Little Richard or Fats Domino, or portraying the youthful exuberance of Rick Nelson, who grew into an embittered veteran whose audience didn't want him to ever change. Picture yourself exhibiting the wildly uninhibited command of the stage that James Brown possessed. All of that is included in Sheree Homer's study.

This book will teach, inspire, enlighten and entertain readers with fascinating stories from people whose love for these great artists is so strong that they have dedicated their existence to keeping their memories alive. Having an expert like Sheree Homer document these stories for future generations will help us better understand and appreciate them all.

James L. Neibaur is a film and media historian and the author of over 30 published books.

Preface

I decided to write a book about tribute artists and not strictly impersonators. There is a difference. Impersonators are people who try to sound and look like the icon they are portraying, while a tribute artist doesn't necessarily look or sound the part, but pays homage to the legendary artist's song catalogue. I am focusing on individuals who do tribute shows, even though there are many out there who showcase the music of bands like The Beatles, Led Zeppelin, The Rolling Stones, etc.

Other books have been written about tribute artists, most notably four by author Bea Fogelman: *Copycats*, *Copycats 2*, *Who's Not Who: Celebrity Impersonators and the People Behind the Curtain* and *Showtime: Directory of Entertainment*. There's also *Living the Life: The World of Elvis Tribute Artists* by Patty Carroll and *Daily Doubles: Celebrity Impersonators* by C.J. Morgan and Jack Bullard. In order to write this book about 40 tribute artists, I conducted numerous interviews and consulted various books and websites. These biographies reveal how they decided to become tribute artists, their first shows and how their fan base has grown, how they have developed as artists, and their challenges transitioning from their portrayals to regular life.

I couldn't uncover more recent statistics, but in 2010, it was estimated that there were 400,000 Elvis Presley tribute artists. Before Presley passed away in 1977, there were a few already popping up around the country, most notably Andy Kaufman, Johnny Harra, Rick Saucedo and Dave Ehlert. The first known ETA (Elvis Tribute Artist) was Carl "Cheesie" Nelson, who started doing his act in 1954 on Texarkana, Arkansas, radio. He even shared the bill with Presley a few times, and it has been said that Presley was a fan.

Elvis Presley Enterprises didn't always welcome Elvis tribute acts. In fact, for years there was a prohibition from dressing like Presley while touring the grounds of Graceland. In 2007, that changed when Elvis Presley Enterprises decided to host the first-ever Ultimate Elvis Tribute Artist Contest and Shawn Klush won the title. It has since become

Preface

a yearly tradition. In this book, three winners are featured: Bill Cherry, Jay Dupuis and Dwight Icenhower.

Other tribute acts pay homage to Buddy Holly, Roy Orbison, Ricky Nelson, Johnny Cash and Jerry Lee Lewis. One of the most popular musicals in recent years, *Million Dollar Quartet*, is based on the December 4, 1956, jam session at Sun Studio in Memphis, Tennessee, that featured Elvis, Carl Perkins, Johnny Cash and Jerry Lee Lewis. While it was on Broadway, Levi Kreis won a Tony for his performance as Lewis. There have been several variations of this stage show since its inception in 2006.

The tribute artist industry has grown in popularity and garnered legions of diehard fans. Besides sold-out theaters, cruise ships have dedicated their itineraries to these portrayals. In 2018, a filmmaker in Canada produced the documentary *Almost Almost Famous*, which focused on the lives of three different tribute acts.

It is important to support the music scene whenever possible. Fans should attend shows and purchase merchandise from the artists. Thanks to all those who continue to pay tribute to legendary performers. You are helping keep their music and memories alive. I never got to see Elvis Presley or Buddy Holly in person, so it's a thrill for me when I get to see a recreation.

ONE

The Rockabilly Hepcat
Elvis Presley

Kavan Hashemian

The musical *Million Dollar Quartet*, based upon the once-in-a-lifetime Sun Studio jam session that featured Elvis Presley, Carl Perkins, Johnny Cash and Jerry Lee Lewis, ran on and off Broadway for several years, and it continues to showcase productions across the country. The best-known actor to portray Presley was Eddie Clendening since he had a stint on Broadway with the show, but several Elvis Tribute Artists have also stepped into the role: Tyler Hunter, Cody Slaughter and Brandon Bennett. Kavan Hashemian joined the cast in 2016. He explained, "Mike Albert recommended me. My theater background was extremely limited before this show, with just a little experience in high school. Learning to play guitar on top of learning the show in two weeks was a crazy thing to do, but I made it through somehow. I'm currently doing my ninth production, with the tenth one lined up. Being thrust into the theater world has really made me more interested in acting beyond the Elvis role. *Million Dollar Quartet* has been a true blessing in my life and career."[1] When not involved with the musical, Hashemian performs around the country with his own tribute to the King of Rock and Roll.

Hashemian was born in 1987 in Columbus, Ohio. He began his singing career at age three: "A local Elvis, Mike Albert, brought me up on stage. I was in a homemade Elvis outfit, made by my grandmother, who was a huge fan. I just vaguely remember a very positive reaction from the crowd. Mike was always kind in bringing me up for a song or two when he'd see me dressed up in the audience. That started when I was three and lasted well into my teenage years. My preparation for playing Elvis started off in a very natural way because for as long as I can remember, I've always been surrounded by his music and movies." Before his initial stage performances, Hashemian practiced his moves

You Sound Just Like...

Kavan Hashemian recreates an iconic Elvis Presley publicity shot from the 1957 movie *Jailhouse Rock* (courtesy Kavan Hashemian).

in front of the TV set in his family's living room. Obviously, Presley tops his list of musical influences, followed by Jack White, John Mayer and The Beatles.

The tent set up during Elvis Week in Memphis gave fans the fantastic opportunity to see ETAs from around the world, and Hashemian graced its stage many times. The first time he played there, one of the songs he sang was "Blue Suede Shoes." During Elvis Week, he met Dean Z: "We met when we were both little. His mother and my grandmother became good friends, and so did we. I've been fortunate to work alongside Dean multiple times throughout the years." Theaters, fairs and festivals are popular venues for Hashemian: "The local shows I do with my backing band are generally 90 minutes to two hours. I've played for crowds that range from 1800 to 2500. A few years back, I sang the 'The Star-Spangled Banner' as Elvis at a baseball game that had several thousand people in attendance."

Typically, he pays tribute to the '50s era of Presley's musical catalogue, but the singer enjoys performing Presley's music from the late '60s and early '70s era the most because those are some of his favorite tunes and because he does it the least. He loves to sing the original 1957 version of "Jailhouse Rock": "[Even though] it is one of the hardest Elvis songs to perform, it's also one of the most fun because of the movements that go along with it and because it always gets a positive reaction from the crowd." As a teenager, he ripped the pants of his "Jailhouse Rock" outfit a few times. "If I Can Dream" is his favorite song to listen to and to see Presley perform, "[because] of the real emotion in it. I always feel emotional when I sing that song as well." He's never had an issue with fulfilling a song request: "I honestly can't remember not being able to perform at least a significant portion. However, there are a few songs that I would need to read the lyrics for, because I don't perform them that often."

For years, his grandmother made his jumpsuits and pieced together '50s- and '60s-style outfits for him to wear. He still has some of them. These days, he frequently shops at both B&K Enterprises and Lansky's. Doing his hair can take anywhere from 20 minutes to an hour, "depending on how cooperative it wants to be on that given day. In my opinion, having to work so much on my hair is the biggest downside. Sometimes I wish I could just shave it all off, but I'm going to use it as long as I have it." Portraying Presley can be quite an adrenaline rush. Hashemian acknowledged, "It usually takes me a while to come down from a show. I relax by doing non–Elvis-related activities like listening to other types of music (anything from blues in the early 1900s to contemporary music), watching a movie, or playing video games." His favorite movies are *King Creole, Change of Habit,* any movie starring Tom Cruise, such as *A Few Good Men* and *Mission: Impossible,* the *Back to the Future* trilogy and *Star Wars.*

Besides his own shows, Hashemian has worked with *Legends in Concert* on several occasions: "My first experience with them was in Myrtle Beach, South Carolina, as a fill-in, doing a strictly '50s set. A few years after that, I worked for them again in Branson, Missouri, doing a set covering the '50s, the '60s movies and the *'68 Comeback Special*." In 2007, he appeared on the TV program, *The World's Greatest Elvis*: "The BBC contacted me and asked if I'd be interested. There were 20 or 30 ETAs from around the world competing on that show. I sang 'Jailhouse Rock' and 'Blue Suede Shoes,' and there were some group numbers." Shawn Klush beat out his fellow competitors and won the prize. Even though Hashemian didn't take home the title, he was crowned The World's #1 Rock and Roll Elvis and wouldn't trade any of his experiences: "My favorite aspect of performing is bringing people joy while getting to do something creative at the same time. Not many people get that instant gratification for their work, so I consider myself very fortunate."

Travis LeDoyt

Typically, rockabilly fans are not keen on tribute artists, but Travis LeDoyt is a hit overseas with ardent fans of the roots music scene. He has performed at the Wildest Cats in Town Weekender and the Hemsby Rock'n'Roll Weekender. They go wild for his portrayal of the King of Rock and Roll. Another festival that loves having him play its stage is the Tupelo Elvis Festival in Tupelo, Mississippi. Thanks to them, he had the opportunity to open for Chuck Berry. He remembered, "As I ended my set, I was told by one of the promoters to keep going as Chuck wouldn't be coming out yet. The festival had provided a band for him, but he'd brought his own bass player and was trying to renegotiate his contracted price, so he could pay his guy. Halfway through my singing of 'A Big Hunk o' Love,' Chuck walked on stage with guitar in hand. I was excited, thinking he would plug into an amp and join in, but unfortunately, that wasn't the case. He said to me, 'It's my turn now,' so we stopped the song suddenly. I then said into the mike, 'Chuck Berry everyone,' and walked offstage."[2]

LeDoyt also opened for Little Richard at a Phoenix, Arizona, show: "I met him in his dressing room backstage where it was understood that we wouldn't be allowed photos. His advice, through our brief encounter, was, 'Keep God close to your heart.'" Sharing the playbill with these

One. The Rockabilly Hepcat

Travis LeDoyt was friends with legendary drummer W.S. Holland. Holland once showed him a plaid jacket that had belonged to Elvis Presley and told LeDoyt that he could wear it for a couple of songs at his Tupelo, Mississippi, show. It was the same jacket that Presley had worn when he was sworn into the Army. LeDoyt recalled, "Even though Elvis was two inches taller than me, it fit great. I felt spiritually close to Elvis" (courtesy Travis LeDoyt).

two artists was memorable but not as much as meeting two of the King's sidemen, Scotty Moore and D.J. Fontana, and recording at Sun Studio.

LeDoyt was born in Greenfield, Massachusetts, in 1977. Even though Elvis Presley's music was played throughout his childhood by his father, he discovered him on his own: "I was flipping through the stations on TV one day and landed on a documentary about Elvis. I couldn't stop watching. I then purchased the 'Sun Sessions' CD, which was the first music I ever bought, and played it over and over until I knew the songs so well [that] I couldn't help but sing along. That discovery is what started me singing at age 16. I don't recall the first song I sang, but it would have been one of those Sun recordings. Interestingly, someone had given me a recording of Ronnie McDowell singing Elvis' songs. That's when I realized it might be possible to sound like Elvis. "It's hard to say what made me gravitate toward Elvis. He had a special quality to his voice that felt magical to me. It stood out and resonated with me. When I really listened, I realized how special he was. I also loved his story of coming from nothing and being discovered."

While attending school, LeDoyt was the class clown: "I had problems focusing and by distracting others, I forced them down to my level. As a middle child, I also loved attention. However, I was never mean or cruel, just goofy. I had been watching a lot of older *Saturday Night Live* episodes and loved when Chevy Chase played President Ford and would fall off a ladder or something, so I would trip over chairs in the lunchroom, get my foot caught in a garbage can, or throw myself down a flight of stairs. It moved beyond the physical antics to impersonating a pizza delivery guy or a custodial engineer, where I would try and repair the heating units in the classroom. The teachers, who didn't know me really, would try and be patient as I interrupted their class to fiddle around with my 'repairs.' I still run into those I graduated with, and they will remind me of some silly prank that I pulled, which I'd forgotten. Elvis was a clown as well, so it's something we both share naturally."

In 1999, LeDoyt began his singing career by performing in the Greenfield High School talent show: "I had friends in the chorus class who knew I was an Elvis 'nut,' and they dared me to do it. In fact, some of them sang back up on the three numbers I did, 'Hound Dog,' 'I Beg of You' and 'Teddy Bear.'" Around the same time, he tried his hand at songwriting: "I recall being excited to share my first tune with the high school music teacher, but he said to me, 'It doesn't really go anywhere.' At the time, I was embarrassed and disheartened, but I kept working at it, and I definitely got better." Since then, he has issued two CDs of original music: *Lonely Street* (2006) and *Musical Time Machine* (2010). The latter was influenced by listening to The Beatles, The Who, Led Zeppelin and Matchbox 20. *Lonely Street* features tunes that LeDoyt wrote in a '50s style: "Though they would fit the sound of my shows, I don't incorporate them. If people come to see an Elvis show, it's my feeling that they don't want to hear something else."

His first professional gig was at the Classic Day Festival in Greenfield, Massachusetts. "I had met a guitarist, who helped me put a three-piece band together. I thought I did rather poorly and was surprised when people gathered around me after the show and asked for business cards and if I had a show schedule. I have videos of those early shows, but I refuse to watch them. I was too nervous and stiff onstage."

In 2004, LeDoyt participated in a stage production of *King Creole*: "For years, I had this idea of performing it on stage because it is my favorite Elvis movie. A good friend of mine, Cathy King, had years of experience producing and directing plays, so we made it happen. I wrote the script from the movie, adding in a couple of scenes. It was a lot of work but remains one of my fondest memories. I believe we ran it for a few weekends locally, and it was very well received."

Around the same time, he met W.S. Holland through connections at the Rockabilly Hall of Fame in Jackson, Tennessee. "We were trying to put together a show with several artists and had recorded an album to sell at that show. I was told we'd record five songs each, and they'd use two of the best. The experience of working with W.S. was an honor and a real high point in my life." Holland also bestowed a special gift onto LeDoyt by letting him wear one of Presley's jackets: "W.S. had shown me the jacket at his house, and he made the offer of letting me wear it for a couple of songs in the upcoming Tupelo show. It was what Elvis had worn when being sworn into the Army. I believe it was toward the end of the show that we had W.S. walk out and explain to the audience how he came into possession of the jacket. Then he put it on me, and we did a few numbers. Even though Elvis was two inches taller than me, it fit great. I felt spiritually close to Elvis, and it's a memory that I'll cherish forever."

These days, LeDoyt stays busy in the States by playing casinos and performing arts centers and gigging on cruises: "Usually I work with my Nashville band, but aboard the ten to twenty cruises I play a year, I am backed by the orchestra provided." He has also been booked to play the Hemsby Rock'n'Roll Weekender in the United Kingdom several times: "I've found the U.K. fans to be very welcoming. They're a lively and wild crowd, and it makes my job much more enjoyable with that sort of reaction. They seem to appreciate the fact that I make the trip over, and they treat me better than I deserve."

Throughout his career, LeDoyt has always made sure to stay true to himself: "I love Elvis and his music, but I don't live and breathe him. My mother told me from the start to never lose sight of who I am, and I haven't. My focus has been studying him on stage and listening carefully to his singing."

In preparation for his shows, he typically likes to have at least an hour to get ready, but he commented, "There have been times I've had only 20 or 30 minutes, which is tough. Once, years ago, we flew in for a gig, and our plane was late. My luggage didn't make it, and I had to run out to buy some clothes and shoes that would at least fit the Elvis image. When I pulled into a K-Mart, there was a bomb scare, so the police blocked it off. I found another clothing store and got back to the theater five minutes before showtime. I did a rush job on the hair and makeup and was literally pulling on my last shoe as I came out from behind the curtain." Since then, he has perfected styling his hair in five minutes: "I use hair gel, hair spray and a hairdryer. I used to use a petroleum-based hair product, and even though it worked great for the stage, it wouldn't wash out for days and was so greasy."

For now, the majority of LeDoyt's setlists feature Presley tunes from the '50s and '60s. He acknowledged, "I'm really enjoying singing some of Elvis' movie songs. Life can seem so dark and heavy at times that they feel like a relief. If only life was like those campy beach movies. I also love his gospel music. Those songs are so moving, so powerful. Since I never know who's attending their first show, seeing me, I feel like I have to do a lot of the number one hits: 'Heartbreak Hotel,' 'Hound Dog,' 'Teddy Bear,' etc. However, just to keep things interesting for me and for those who have seen many of my shows, I like to add more obscure songs into the mix, such as 'Kiss Me Quick' and 'You Don't Know Me.' I haven't studied the '70s very much, not because I don't care for it, but because I don't want to be burned out before I've even had a chance to perform it. There's no doubt that I will, at some point, move into that era. Recently, I've begun performing in the black leather from the *'68 Comeback Special*. I've had many requests for songs I didn't know. Sometimes people request songs that Elvis didn't do, but they think he did. Other times, they will ask for obscure songs that I know, but the band doesn't. One that comes to mind is 'Big Boots' from *G.I. Blues*. Since I don't yet do the '70s Elvis, when people ask for 'An American Trilogy' or 'Burning Love,' I have to turn them down. My favorite thing about what I do is when I can bring a fan back to their youth or a time when they saw Elvis. Also, when someone tells me that they weren't really an Elvis fan, but they are now."

Caden Gamblin

For tribute artists, there is an element of acting involved in an accurate representation. Therefore, it is always helpful if they have a theater background. Caden Gamblin has taken on the role of Elvis Presley in both the ETA world as well as two different productions: *Cash, Killer, and King*, co-starring Neil Morrow, and *Sun Records: A Million Dollar Story*, which was a 90-minute production put together by Michael Monroe Goodman. "Michael contacted me on social media and asked if I wanted to do the gig," Gamblin recalled, "and of course I said yes."[3] The show took place in a theater in Old Tucson. Carl Perkins, Roy

One. The Rockabilly Hepcat

Orbison, Elvis Presley and June and Johnny Cash were all depicted. Gamblin's regular gig is performing as a stuntman at Old Tucson. The movie studio-theme park has an illustrious past. Since 1939, many films have been partially shot there, including *Winchester '73*, *Rio Bravo* and *Tombstone*.

Caden Gamblin was born in Tucson, Arizona, on May 24, 2000. His father introduced him to Presley's music by playing his records. When Gamblin heard "Can't Help Falling in Love" on the radio, he fell in love with it. At 16, he started his singing career, and the first song he sang and played guitar on was "That's All Right." His premiere gig took place at an assisted living home, and he was a hit. "I prepared for the role by watching videos on YouTube. One thing that I really gravitated toward was Elvis' charisma." He also likes many independent singers and bands, including Cage the Elephant, Arctic Monkeys and The Growlers: "Some of their music can sound very retro at times but with a modern twist."

His father had introduced him to Elvis Presley's music, but it was hearing "Can't Help Falling in Love" on the radio that changed Caden Gamblin's life forever. In only three short years in his tribute to the King of Rock and Roll, Gamblin has already won a few competitions, including the E.P. Expo in Yuma, Arizona, and the Elvis Rocks Mesquite in Nevada (courtesy Caden Gamblin).

Gamblin sometimes plays at a local diner on Fridays and Saturdays, but typically he does shows all over the country and in Canada: "The crowds are pretty great in Canada. You'd be surprised how many Elvis fans are up there." His shows average from 90 minutes to over two hours. He chooses a mix of hits and more obscure ones because he likes to introduce people to songs they may not have heard. "My favorite Elvis songs to sing are his early ones, from the '50s and '60s. I would say my favorite era to portray is the 1950s, especially 1957. I also enjoy doing the *'68 Comeback Special* sit-down session because it's different and gives a little more variety, but I think I'm known for my '50s portrayal. Sometimes people suggest songs that I don't know the lyrics to. I'm just very polite and tell them I don't know the song very well and ask if they have another."

Gamblin acknowledged, "I get my clothes at Lansky's, B&K Enterprises, and believe it or not, eBay. Sometimes places like that have excellent stuff for cheap." Styling his hair usually takes between 15 and 20 minutes. "I use three to four different hair products." After the shows, he said that he usually can't relax and is very tired. To regain his energy, he sits and drinks a lot of water.

He added, "I have won a few contests such as the E.P. Expo in Yuma, Arizona, in 2019 and the Elvis Rocks Mesquite in Nevada, in June 2018. [The latter's prize was $3000.] I have competed in a few Ultimate preliminaries, but those contests are a bit more difficult. I'm going to keep trying, though." His parents have been very supportive: "They are very protective too and want what's best for me." Some advice that he has taken to heart is "to only watch Elvis. Do not try to be like other ETAs; just be true to Elvis and be yourself. Also, don't let your head get too big." Gamblin says his goal in performing is to make everyone happy. "If they're not happy, neither am I."[4]

Ricky Aron

Cliff Richard was England's answer to Elvis Presley, so it's not surprising that an Elvis Tribute Artist, Ricky Aron, was a natural choice to play Richard in *Cliff the Musical*. In 2003, after being suggested by the backing band, Aron auditioned and got the part. The show was performed for three months in London's West End, then toured England for another two months. After that, they entertained audiences in Denmark for two weeks. These days, Aron's primary tributes are Elvis Presley and Shakin' Stevens. Stevens has not seen Aron's homage, but he did see Aron in *Cliff the Musical*: "[Stevens] came backstage, and we had a chat," said Aron.[5] Aron typically plays in England, but he has gigged in Memphis, Tennessee, and Dallas, Texas: "The crowds in the U.S. scream more. U.K. crowds are a little more reserved."

Ricky Aron was born in 1978 in Liverpool, England. At age five, he began singing. It was a Shakin' Stevens tune but he doesn't remember which one. When Aron was 14, he performed for the first time on stage.

One. The Rockabilly Hepcat

It was a school concert where he sang "Johnny B. Goode" and "Love Me." For the latter, he dressed as Elvis Presley in his G.I. uniform. Aron acknowledged, "Elvis caught my attention at a very early age. We always had his music playing in our house."

Aron's parents helped him develop his love for Presley and roots music: "My dad sang his favorite Elvis songs. When an Elvis movie would come on TV, I would always get really excited. It was like a special occasion. I'd sit and stare at him, and to this day, I still do that. He has a way of hooking you in, and once he has you, he doesn't let go."

In 2006, Aron made his premiere performance as an Elvis Tribute Artist: "Preparing for the role is not something I've ever done. I actually never wanted to be an ETA. It just happened. People would say, 'You sound like Elvis; you should sing more,' so I did, and fortunately, it paid off." His favorite songs to perform are "You'll Never Walk Alone" and "Just Pretend": "They are both challenging songs, and 'You'll Never Walk Alone' means a lot to me. In my set, I always have to include the hits, but if I know there are diehard fans in the crowd, there will be a lot more obscure songs since they're my favorites."

Aron's main gig as Shakin' Stevens is the yearly fan party in Birmingham, England. "I was a Shaky fan before I was an Elvis fan. At a young age, he was the coolest thing I had ever seen. His movements were unbelievable, and I would practice every day to get as close to them as I could. I've seen Shaky over 40 times in concert. The most memorable was my first at the age of seven in 1985.

Ricky Aron was a fan of Shakin' Stevens before becoming aware of Elvis Presley's music. These days, he pays tribute to both. He has seen Shakin' Stevens more than 40 times. The most memorable for him was his first at age seven (courtesy Ricky Aron).

My parents kept it a secret and told me we were off to see a pantomime. When we arrived, there were screaming girls everywhere, waving their Shaky flags and scarves. It was then I realized I'd be seeing Shaky for the first time. Thirty-five years later, and I'm still as big a Shaky fan as I was then. He is definitely the reason why I wanted to become an entertainer." Aron's other musical influences are Chris Isaak and Robbie Williams.

Theaters, hotels and private events make up the majority of Aron's schedule. His largest audience was 10,000 people in Italy. He has also performed at several ETA festivals across the United Kingdom and Europe. He has received quite a few accolades, including 2007's Europe's Best '50s Elvis; champion in 2015's Europe's Tribute to Elvis, which qualified him for the Ultimate Elvis Contest in Memphis; and champion in 2018's Danish Elvis Festival. While those have certainly been career highlights, he's had his embarrassing moments, too, such as the time he fell off the stage during a sound check: "I damaged all the ligaments in my ankle and passed out shortly afterward. I then had to be stretchered out of the venue with some guy asking me what I did for an encore." The adoring crowds help Aron to continue to spread the music of Presley and Stevens. He loves what he does, even describing life as an ETA as the best job in the world. He will forever remember these words spoken to him by comedian Ken Dodd: "Always try to enjoy your time on stage. Once you stop enjoying it, it's time to stop."

Jake Slater

In 2009, Jake Slater won the Early Years segment of the Saginaw Kingfest. Two years later, he won the title of King of Saginaw; he won it again in 2014. His most outstanding achievement thus far came in 2019 when he placed in the Top Five at the Ultimate ETA Competition in Memphis.

His career as an Elvis Tribute Artist began at 16. Slater naturally gravitated toward Elvis because, as he revealed, "I thought Elvis was such a magnetic person—his personality and his talent."[6]

Slater was born on December 31, 1991, in Saginaw, Michigan: "I'm a Capricorn like Elvis, which I've always thought was really neat." At age six, he started singing. At this time, Slater became a Presley fan, having heard "(You're So Square) Baby I Don't Care" on his grandparents' radio. He commented, "It was such a unique song and attention-grabber. I then dove into all that I could find." His other favorite singers include Dean Martin, Perry Como, Carl Perkins, Jerry Lee Lewis and Ricky Nelson.

One. The Rockabilly Hepcat

In 2019, Jake Slater placed in the Top Five at the Ultimate ETA Competition in Memphis. In the final round, he impressed the judges with rousing renditions of "A Fool Such as I" and "Stuck on You" (courtesy Jake Slater).

You Sound Just Like...

In 2007, Slater performed at a Christmas party for a small group of family, neighbors and close friends. (The only other times he had ever sung were for his parents in their living room. Incidentally, they are his biggest supporters.) He revealed, "I sang a little of everything—[Elvis] and, of course, Christmas songs. My first real booking was at a Military Club in the summer of 2008, thanks to one of the party's attendees, Jean Ann Gordon." The show was sold out, and the audience's warm reception gave Slater the boost in confidence that he needed to continue.

These days, Slater performs Presley songs from the '50s, '60s and '70s. He revealed, "I'd have to say my favorite to perform is early to mid–60s. When I was younger, I was shyer but ... like anything, the more you perform and get used to it, the more comfortable you become." His shows range from one to two hours: "The biggest shows I've done have been sold-out casino shows with anywhere from a thousand to 3000 in attendance. I even played a fairground where 5000 fans attended." Slater features the classic hits but also sets time aside for the rarer cuts. Some of the tunes that top his setlists are "Stuck on You," "Baby, What You Want Me to Do," "(You're So Square) Baby I Don't Care" and "Baby, Let's Play House." After a show, Slater, still full of energy, will sit in his garage and listen to records or watch TV. "My favorite aspect of performing is seeing the joy on people's faces, bringing back memories for those who were lucky enough to have seen him live, and building new memories for those who didn't.

I chose to be an Elvis Tribute Artist out of sheer admiration for the man. He was such an amazing and magnetic performer; also such a great human being and humanitarian.... I want to do the best and most respectful tribute I can to the man who brought so much to the world!"[7]

Finley Watkins

Elvis Tribute Artist Finley Watkins has expanded his repertoire to also include the music of Jerry Lee Lewis, Buddy Holly, Carl Perkins, Johnny Cash and Elton John. However, "Elvis is my favorite because I like his music and style the most."[8] The young singer has performed in Las Vegas and Memphis and has shared stages with Narvel Felts, Ronnie McDowell, Mickey Gilley and Johnny Lee. Paying tribute to other artists is what Watkins is known for, but he has recently begun writing original tunes. One of his compositions won second place at the University of Missouri Song Writing Competition.

Finley Watkins was born on July 31, 2008, in Poplar Bluff, Missouri.

One. The Rockabilly Hepcat

At age four, Watkins began singing. Around the same time, he also picked up the guitar. The first Elvis song he sang on stage was "Heartbreak Hotel." He recalled, "I performed two songs that day. The crowds loved me because I was little and liked Elvis." At the age of six, he entertained audiences at the tent during Elvis Week; he sang "Blue Suede Shoes," "Trouble" and "Hound Dog."

Watkins became a Presley fan after looking him up on YouTube: "I liked his look, his music, his movements and his outfits ... everything about him." Besides Presley, his musical influences include Jerry Lee Lewis, Buddy Holly, James Burton and Scotty Moore. Presley is also on his list of favorite singers, along with Freddie Mercury, Elton John and Johnny Cash.

The teenager doesn't find it challenging to juggle getting an education with performing: "[But] my school is super-strict with attendance, so when I miss, it counts against me and keeps me from doing stuff. I am an A student, and last year I was the top academic student in the fourth grade at my school. [However,] I do not like school because kids don't get me."

The Elvis Tribute Artists community is a tight-knit group of ladies and gentlemen who treat one another like family. They support and encourage each other, and there is no jealousy among them. Watkins is one of the youngest to pay homage to the King of Rock and Roll, and two fellow ETAs

When young Elvis impersonator Finley Watkins was interviewed by a newspaper, a member of Ellen DeGeneres' staff read it and then contacted him to ask if he would appear on her show. He sang "Blue Suede Shoes" and had a short chat with DeGeneres (courtesy Finley Watkins).

have gone out of their way to be kind to him. In March 2021, Dean Z presented Watkins with a gift, a replica of Presley's Egyptian Pharaoh jumpsuit, including the cape and belt. A few months later, at the Tupelo Elvis Festival, Cody Slaughter invited Watkins to jam in the hotel lobby. Another highlight was when Watkins sang on stage while Linda Thompson, Presley's former girlfriend, sat spellbound in the audience. Thompson has become a fan of many of the ETAs.

Lance Lipinsky is another artist who has occasionally shared the spotlight with Watkins. "I first met Lance at an Elvis show in Illinois," said Watkins. "I talked to him while he signed a picture for me, and then he had me sing a little for him. The next time I saw him was at his show in Memphis. He saw me in the audience and knew I could play piano because I think Dean Z's sister had sent him a video. He then invited me on stage to perform with him. I did a couple of songs on the keyboard and then an Elvis song with him and his band. The most memorable moment was at the after-party during Elvis Week when he said he wanted me to play with him, and if they wouldn't let me, then he wasn't playing." The promoter allowed both to perform.

Festivals, restaurants, theaters and hotels are Watkins' typical venues. "My show is two hours—the first hour is Elvis, and then the second is a variety. The largest audience I ever played for was 2000 people in Las Vegas." He chooses his setlists according to where he's performing and according to what he thinks the crowd would like; he always includes "That's All Right" and "Hound Dog." His aunt creates his clothes: "It takes about a week for her to sew them. My favorite is the '70s Sundial two-piece suit." After his performances, Watkins talks to fans, poses for photos and signs autographs.

On the January 11, 2017, *Ellen DeGeneres Show*, he sang "Blue Suede Shoes." He remembered, "I had done an interview for a local newspaper that went national. One of her staff saw it and contacted me. After weeks of interviews, I found out I was selected. I never get nervous, but that time I was because I was going to be on national TV and meet Ellen. She seemed to like the tribute and my guitar playing." When he finished, she presented him with an Elvis jumpsuit. Three years later, on May 17, 2020, Watkins made his second television appearance when he performed "Whole Lotta Shakin' Goin' On" on *Little Big Shots*. Jerry Lee Lewis, who gave fame to that song, has even given his stamp of approval. After catching Watkins' act in Millington, Tennessee, Lewis said, "He has it! He is gonna be a star!"[9]

Two

"Rave On" for Me
Buddy Holly

Johnny Rogers

Tribute artists typically limit themselves to portraying one artist, maybe two. Johnny Rogers is an exception. His résumé is wide-ranging, with similarities in his vocals and mannerisms to Buddy Holly, Elvis Presley, Prince, Waylon Jennings, Dean Martin and many others. He uses pickup bands in the three different shows that he does around the world. *Buddy and Beyond: The History of Rock 'n' Roll* is his most popular concert: He starts with his tribute to Holly, then moves on to Roy Orbison, Jerry Lee Lewis, Ricky Nelson, Chuck Berry and others before closing out his performance with the music of Presley.

Since 1982, Rogers has been captivating audiences with his versatility. Some of his career highlights were the occasions when he played for U.S. Presidents George Bush, George W. Bush, Bill Clinton and Barack Obama and his 2016 induction into the Iowa Rock 'n Roll Music Association's Hall of Fame.

Johnny Rogers was born on June 5, 1967, in Jackson, Tennessee. His father, a disc jockey and music promoter, was acquainted with some of the biggest names in show business, such as Elvis Presley, Johnny Cash, George Jones, Lefty Frizzell and Conway Twitty. Therefore, music was at the forefront for Rogers at an early age. Every Sunday after church, there was a country music jam session at his house. Lester Flatt, Earl Scruggs and Jerry Lee Lewis would stop by. Lewis showed the young Rogers a few things on the guitar, even though the boy really wasn't interested in playing at that time. Rogers' father had bought him the guitar, but he'd rather hide it under his bed than practice.

Rogers didn't become enthralled with music until he heard Buddy Holly sing "Rave On" on the soundtrack of the movie *American Hot*

You Sound Just Like...

The first Buddy Holly song that Johnny Rogers ever heard was "Rave On." He instantly became a fan and knew that somehow Holly would be part of his destiny: "I was born to be Buddy. It all came naturally" (courtesy Johnny Rogers).

Wax: "It was like a switch turned on, and I was hooked."[1] A 15-year-old high schooler, Rogers began playing the guitar. He was primarily self-taught, except for a few chords his father had taught him, and the first song he learned was "Peggy Sue." He then immersed himself into

Holly's catalogue and even began dressing the part, which included wearing thick black horn-rimmed glasses.

Hoping to perform publicly, he sought out local honky-tonks. He was allowed entry, thanks in part to a fake I.D. His father was good friends with Jimmy Nichols, which led to a gig at the Off Broadway Lounge where Rogers played lead guitar. The first songs he played with him were "Peggy Sue" and "That'll Be the Day." Rogers stayed with Nichols for six years before he branched off on his own.

These days, Rogers is primarily known for his spot-on homage to Holly, which is endorsed by the Holly family. One of Rogers' dearest friends, Tommy Allsup, who played guitar for Holly on his final tour, remarked that Rogers "has the aura of Buddy about him."[2] Rogers even acknowledged, "I was born to be Buddy. It all came naturally, like a hand in a glove." However, Rogers showcases his talents in three different productions: *Buddy and Beyond: The History of Rock 'n' Roll*, *Legends of Country Music* and *The Purple One Lives On*. A typical performance is 90 minutes in length. "I prefer not to use a setlist because that way every show is different; however, I always perform the artists' biggest hits." He's had requests for songs that he didn't know: "I just perform a different song from the same artist. I know thousands of songs, including over 300 of my own." His musical influences are Holly, Presley, Hank Williams Sr., Jimi Hendrix, Prince and Dean Martin. Rogers is a third cousin to Presley on his mother's side, but never met him.

Whether it's paying tribute to numerous artists or honoring his material, "normal" life is music: "I have met many of my heroes, and they always told me to be true to myself and my music, to never compromise on either." It takes him two hours or more to come down from the natural high of entertaining: "I usually return to my room and create more music." Rogers admitted, "Music is in my blood. I am music, and music is me."[3]

John Mueller

In 1992, John Mueller portrayed Buddy Holly in a play named *Be Bop a Lula* for the first time. That show led to a four-year run in *Buddy: The Buddy Holly Story*.

Then Mueller branched out and created the *Winter Dance Party* production. Since 1999, he has recreated the famous 1959 tour of the same name, gigging at many of the venues that Holly, Ritchie Valens and The Big Bopper played before their tragic deaths in a plane crash. All three families of the estates endorse the show. During the one-hour 45-minute concert, Mueller, Ray Anthony as Valens and Linwood Sasser as The Big Bopper sing the three stars' hits. In the sets, Mueller also incorporates a song he has written in tribute to Holly, "Hey Buddy," a tune that only took him two weeks to compose.

Holly has changed Mueller's life, and it all began at a young age when he was introduced to rock and roll through his older brother's record collection. Holly, Chuck Berry, Little Richard, Fats Domino, The Everly Brothers, Elvis Presley, Eddie Cochran, Johnny Cash, Carl Perkins and Jerry Lee Lewis became musical influences. However, Mueller's favorite singer is Nat King Cole, whose voice he described as "smooth as silk."[4]

Around age four, Mueller picked up a guitar and started singing: "I even made up my own song called 'When the Cowboy Plays His Practice.' My brother George was instrumental in my musical development. A child prodigy guitarist reading and playing off sheet music by seven years old, he took me to my first concert—a Doc Watson show. I was so blown away by Doc's talent. Blindness did not stop him from being an incredible guitar picker and what a voice [he had]." That concert and his brother's record collection inspired Mueller to teach himself more chords on the guitar. He later took a few lessons at the Old Town School of Folk Music in Chicago.

While in his teens, Mueller discovered a new passion—acting— and he put his music on the back burner and headed to Chicago. While there, he helped found the Raven Theatre Company and studied dramatics with Tom Irwin at the Steppenwolf Theatre. Mueller commented, "Theater was a great [teaching tool on] how to be relaxed in front of an audience and how to find your true voice. Having studied with some great acting teachers, the main thing I learned was preparation is everything." After seven years in Chicago, he relocated to Hollywood, hoping that bigger opportunities would come his way. Television beckoned, and he was cast in minor roles on *Ellen*, *Lois and Clark: The New Adventures of Superman* and *Days of Our Lives*.

Music re-entered Mueller's life when he auditioned for the role of Buddy Holly in the play *Be Bop a Lula*: "I prepared by watching the documentary *The Real Buddy Holly Story* and by reading everything [about Buddy] that I could get my hands on, including Bill Griggs' *Buddy Holly Day-by-Day* booklets." Incidentally, his favorite recordings of Holly's are the ones that he cut alone in his apartment with just his acoustic

Two. "Rave On" for Me

John Mueller initially portrayed Buddy Holly in the play *Be Bop a Lula*. However, after years of doing eight shows a week, he grew weary and decided to try something new. He recreated the *Winter Dance Party* tour, revisiting many of the same ballrooms Holly, Ritchie Valens and The Big Bopper had played. On its first run, he was joined by the original drummer on that tour, Carl Bunch, and former Cricket Niki Sullivan (courtesy John Mueller).

guitar—in particular, "That Makes It Tough," "That's What They Say," "Peggy Sue Got Married," "Learning the Game" and "Crying, Waiting, Hoping." *Be Bop a Lula* was produced by Adam Ant and the Doors' drummer John Densmore and showcased at a small Hollywood theater called Theatre/Theater. James Intveld served as musical director.

After its short run, Mueller answered an ad for an open casting call. He remembered, "Hallmark Cards, who owned American Heartland Theatre in Kansas City, Missouri, had put out a national talent search [for *Buddy: The Buddy Holly Story*]. I sent a video of me singing a few songs and improvising some dialogue. They cast me right away, and it was a fabulous experience."

Buddy: The Buddy Holly Story opened in January 1996 in Kansas City, and Mueller won a Drama Desk Award for Best Actor. "It broke all their box office records and was a big hit," Mueller said. "A producer saw me and brought the show to San Diego, then to Chicago's Apollo Theater for a long run." In 1997, Robert Oliphant came up to Mueller after his performance at the Apollo and said, "You need to have these," handing him a pair of FAOSA frames like Holly wore. Mueller recalled, "[Robert] had bought them in college in 1959." Mueller has worn them since and feels they are an integral part of his authentic portrayal: "They are so well made that they have not broken." The next city to host the musical was Toronto, for two summers: "However, after four years of doing eight shows a week, I was getting pretty tired, and the play was hard on my voice." In fact, Mueller once lost his ability to vocalize: "It was very scary, and I never felt more powerless. It took weeks for me to get it back fully. I have learned to hydrate, breathe in steam every morning, and drink tea."

Mueller now wanted to move on to another venture: "All the reviewers had said the [*Buddy Holly Story*] script was kind of weak, but the last 45 minutes, which was music from the *Winter Dance Party* tour, was great. I got an idea and thought, well, let's just make the music. [Mueller created the *Winter Dance Party* concert experience in 1999.] A friend [had suggested] that we revisit the original ballrooms of the 1959 *Winter Dance Party* and do it in the exact same order as they had, [and we did]. That first tour featured Carl Bunch and Niki Sullivan. Niki was tops. He was an underrated talent and man. He really helped me learn things about Buddy that are not in the books. I miss him greatly. That first run was grueling, but we made so many friends and fans, and the venues kept asking us to come back every year." Besides the original venues, casinos, performing arts centers and theaters have hired them.

Two. "Rave On" for Me

The Riverside Ballroom in Green Bay, Wisconsin, and the Surf Ballroom in Clear Lake, Iowa, have been two of the most frequented tour stops. Mueller recalled, "We played the Surf for the fortieth anniversary of the *Winter Dance Party*. We went to the crash site after the show, too, at one o'clock in the morning. It was freezing cold but well worth it, to pay our respects."

He added, "My favorite place is the Riverside Ballroom. The crowd is not gathered there for a social event [but rather] to rock and celebrate the music and history. When I was dancing with Maria Elena Holly on stage at the Riverside, during the solo section of 'True Love Ways,' she turned, whispered in my ear, and said, 'You have two left feet just like Buddy did.'" In 2005, Maria Elena recommended that Mueller sing at the Rock and Roll Hall of Fame, as part of a tribute that took place after someone was inducted: "It was a night of Buddy's music performed by his peers, surviving band members, and special guests. Tommy Allsup, Marshall Crenshaw, John Mellencamp, Joe Ely and many other greats were there. It was an unforgettable evening."

Throughout the years, the *Winter Dance Party* has featured various individuals who have portrayed Valens and The Big Bopper, most notably Ernie Valens, Ritchie's cousin, and Jay Perry Richardson Jr., The Big Bopper's son. Sadly, in recent years, both have passed away. Mueller's brother was also a regular but has since retired due to all the traveling: "George was a large part of its success. A stickler for details and authenticity, he added an element of guitar mastery and feel for the songs. He knew what to play and when to rock out or lay back."

In 2006, Mueller played on a special limited-edition CD, produced by Scott Porter, at Norman Petty's studio in Clovis, New Mexico. Tommy Allsup, Larry Welborn and Jack Neal were a few other artists who starred on it. Mueller said, "The CD, *That'll Be the Day*, featured mostly songs from Buddy's catalogue. We shot the video for my song 'Hey Buddy' there too. It was a thrill being in that studio. The place is magical."

The *Winter Dance Party* is just one of Mueller's many projects. He also keeps active with the *One Night in Memphis* show, in which he often portrays Carl Perkins: "I created the show as I wanted to have a small side project that featured me more as a band member than the main performer. Our first show was in 2005 at the Corn Palace in South Dakota. I'm so fortunate to have the people that I do in my shows. The band members and performers are all first-rate. The venues always comment on how professional we are to work with." He also keeps busy songwriting and issuing solo albums: "I started writing a real complete song in my late teens, early twenties. Before that, it was nothing anyone would want to hear. Music usually comes to me first, and then I sing along with some made-up improvised lines until I decide what the song is about." In 2020, he released *You Are Here*: "Spotify and YouTube have exposed my music to so many new listeners. My goal now is for a new LP [to be released] every year. I sing my original music around L.A. sometimes but not very frequently as I am out on the road a lot."

Mueller recognizes that he has gained the most notoriety as Holly: "I've reached a bigger audience and done more of his music than he ever had the opportunity to…. I'm honored to be able to do that, but I'm sad that he wasn't able to fully enjoy his creative genius because of this tragic accident."[5]

Three

"It'll Be Me"

Jerry Lee Lewis

Luke Stroud

Jerry Lee Lewis's wild abandon lit Luke Stroud's fuse: "He is my main influence. When I got a Jerry Lee Lewis cassette tape from my mom and dad, it sparked electricity into me. That led me to check out Sun Records and become a collector of vinyl. My most prized 45 is my Sun [copy] of Elvis' 'Good Rockin' Tonight.' I listened to blues that Sam Phillips recorded, and other artists like Roy Orbison, Johnny Cash, Carl Perkins and Elvis Presley."[1] Stroud's first concert was Conway Twitty while his mother was pregnant with him: "She said I jumped when the drums started kicking." The music bug didn't bite until he was 14. As far as bookings, he doesn't seek them out; promoters contact *him*. His fondest performance experiences are the times he shared the stage with Sonny Burgess.

Stroud was born on July 20, 1980, in Newport, Arkansas. Singing began at an early age, alongside his dad at the Freewill Baptist Church in Cave City, Arkansas: "I remember we sang 'Swing Low, Sweet Chariot.' That seemed to go over well. I've been told that the song leader said that I was the only one singing in key." Gospel was the main influence, but there was country too: "My mother liked listening to the radio. I remember hearing Willie Nelson's 'On the Road Again' a lot. Eighties country [on the] radio was all I had been exposed to back then, so when my mom and dad gave me a cassette tape of Jerry Lee [Lewis's Mercury recordings] when I was nine years old, I fell in love with what I was hearing. The first three songs on the tape were 'Great Balls of Fire,' 'Flip, Flop, and Fly' and 'What'd I Say.' They were raw, explosive, and sounded out of control. I went running and jumping throughout the house because it made me so excited. I turned to my dad and said, 'Get me more stuff by *this* guy.' I love good old country music, but that stuff

You Sound Just Like...

Luke Stroud had the opportunity to share the stage many times with Sonny Burgess. The first time came as a complete but pleasant surprise to both Stroud and his band. They were playing the Watermelon Festival in Cave City, Arkansas, and at the end of his set Burgess came on stage unannounced, plugged in his guitar, and just started playing. That night, they jammed together on "Hang Up My Rock and Roll Shoes" and "Whole Lotta Shakin' Goin' On" (photograph by Kris Caraway; courtesy Luke Stroud).

(rockabilly–rock and roll) was what I wanted to play. I felt the most connection with it."

Stroud added, "Then the movie *Great Balls of Fire* came out, and I loved it. I had a piano in the house and pretended to play like Jerry Lee. I turned the lights off and gave a Jerry Lee Lewis show. I poured water on the keys to make the glissandi easier. I literally tore that piano up."

Working hard at perfecting his performances, Stroud caught the attention of one of his high school classmates: "He told the music teacher that I could play like Jerry Lee." In March 1995, when he was 14, Stroud decided that he wanted to properly learn how to play the piano, not just mimic his hero. He explained, "I told my dad to get me a piano that worked as I was ready to learn. I would listen to Jerry Lee and try to figure out the left and the right hand. The first song I learned was 'Cool, Cool Ways' aka 'Sexy Ways.' I spent eight to 15 hours a day teaching myself how to play. Mom and Dad were really supportive. I had started

Three. "It'll Be Me"

in March, and by August, I performed a 19-minute medley of his songs at the Cave City Watermelon Festival [in Cave City, Arkansas]. That night, they really screamed for 'Great Balls of Fire.' I came off stage and told my dad, 'That was fun, so much fun.' The crowd really liked it."

For over 25 years, festivals, nightclubs and private events in and around Arkansas have sought out Stroud: "I let bookings come to me, so I don't play any one place a lot, except for the Cave City Watermelon Festival." He played their annual event for years. One year, an estimated 5000 people were in attendance. Stroud has also wowed audiences at the historic Louisiana Hayride in Shreveport, Louisiana, the Jerry Lee Lewis Café and Honky Tonk in Memphis, the Jerry Lee Lewis Ranch in Nesbit, Mississippi, and the Johnny Cash Heritage Festival in Dyess, Arkansas. The latter's proceeds went toward preserving Cash's boyhood home. Those experiences rank high on his list as unforgettable.

One incident he'd like to forget happened on the way to a gig at the Miner's Day Festival in Cushman, Arkansas: "My dad took a curve too quickly and dumped my Baldwin RPI into the road. It broke into six different pieces. I was fuming mad, but we picked up the pieces and drove to the festival. The main part, a full 88 keys, was intact except for some skid marks on it. The legs, pedal part and other boards were demolished. I got electrical tape and wrapped the power cord, then I sat the main part of the keyboard on the tailgate of my dad's little red Mazda, and I performed my show. I played just like nothing had happened."

His shows are generally 45 minutes in length, and he doesn't use a setlist: "I never know which song I'll start with. I don't know until my hands touch the keys. I like spontaneity, so I don't practice with my band. I play Hank [Williams] Sr., Chuck Berry, Little Richard, Mickey Gilley, etc., usually in the style of Jerry Lee. I have a few tunes that I have written that I throw in every now and then, like 'Woman, I'm Still Thinking of You.' My dad and I wrote one called 'Stepping on the Pieces of My Broken Heart.' I played it with Sonny Burgess at the Silver Moon, and he liked it. We also wrote a song called 'The Heart of Rock'n'Roll,' about Jerry Lee's audition at Sun Studio, but I haven't played it live yet. My favorites are usually the fast boogie-woogie tunes—'Great Balls of Fire,' 'Whole Lotta Shakin' Goin' On' and 'Blue Suede Shoes.'" He'll also toss in more obscure songs, including "Why Should I Cry Over You." Stroud revealed, "I jump around and try to create something that can excite the people that are watching. I don't like over-the-top antics, but getting on top of the piano is part of it."

Lewis has never seen Stroud perform live, but his cousin Mickey

Gilley hired Stroud to be his opening act. However, he has met Lewis: "My mom, dad and I went to his house for his 62nd birthday party. Mickey Gilley, James Burton, Kenny Lovelace and B.B. Cunningham were all there. Jerry Lee came out brandishing a pistol and chopped up his piano-shaped cake with his hand. Jerry Lee played a little keyboard while Mickey sang. Later, Jerry Lee was down by his car collection building, so we went to see him. He was having a good time entertaining the crowd, but he eventually took my notepad and signed it."

On August 30, 2009, at a memorial show for Billy Lee Riley, Stroud shared the bill with Dale Hawkins, Ace Cannon, Carl Mann, Sleepy LaBeef and Sonny Burgess. From 2010 to 2012, Stroud played with Burgess in a band called Jeannie and the Guys: "I had met Sonny in Newport, Arkansas, in 2000. My dad and I just went up to him and started talking. My dad was my manager, and he was asking Sonny about overseas gigs. A few months later, we saw Sonny at Riverside Park in Batesville, Arkansas. I had mentioned how I would like to have one of the Sun Records hats. After his show, Sonny gave me his Sun hat. He was generous like that. I opened for him and the Pacers at the Cave City Watermelon Festival the next time I saw him. [During my set,] he came onstage, plugged in his guitar and just started playing with us on 'Hang Up My Rock and Roll Shoes' and 'Whole Lotta Shakin' Goin' On.' My guitar player was flabbergasted and starstruck. Sonny's guitar sounded so good that night. He often came and played shows with me as my guitar player. I can't remember the last time I played with him, but it was probably at the Silver Moon in 2014. He was so cool to hang out with. I really miss him."

Stroud loves performing, especially for his mom and his fiancée Lacy, whom he met at a Burgess show. His dad took pleasure in seeing the crowds' reactions to his son's boisterous shows. (He passed away from COVID in 2020.) Stroud acknowledged, "I had the greatest parents that I could have ever asked for. They encouraged me to the hilt, and I could never repay them. God blessed me. I never thought I was a good singer until people started coming up to me after shows and telling me what a great singer I was. I've also been told many times that I'm better than Jerry Lee, but that's certainly not my opinion."

Jared Freiburg

Thanks to the stage productions *Million Dollar Quartet, One Night in Memphis* and *The Killer Live: A Tribute to Jerry Lee Lewis,* Jared

Three. "It'll Be Me"

In the seventh grade, Jared Freiburg was introduced to Jerry Lee Lewis's music when his choir teacher gave him and his male chorus a warm-up piece entitled "Great Balls of Fire." The lyrics didn't speak to Freiburg the way the boogie-woogie piano-playing did. After class, he asked the teacher who the original artist was (courtesy Jared Freiburg).

Freiburg gets to channel his inner "wild child" persona. One reviewer commented, "Freiburg ... is a stunningly talented pianist ... beating the upright piano on which he plays as though it owes him money; Freiburg uses hands and feet, head and tail to assault the poor instrument again and again as he pirouettes through a morass of high-energy numbers like a premier danseur."[2] Lewis has even praised his tribute: "Jerry has always been very appreciative of what I do and has on occasion thanked me for carrying [on the torch of] rock and roll."[3] Freiburg's other musical influences include Ray Charles, Elvis Presley, Oscar Peterson, Harry

You Sound Just Like...

Connick Jr., Led Zeppelin, The Beatles, Michael Jackson, Billy Joel and Stevie Wonder.

Freiburg was born on September 12, 1996, in Des Moines, Iowa. His parents separated when he was five, so he spent a lot of long weekends at his grandparents' house: "At their place, there was a lot of '50s music. It started with crooners—Dean Martin, Frank Sinatra, Perry Como, Bobby Darin, etc. I found a liking for that type of sound." Around the same time, his grandmother piqued his interest in the piano: "She had a nice upright in the living room of her house where she taught me simple little things that could be played with one hand. The first song I learned was 'Peter, Peter, Pumpkin Eater.' I seemed to pick things up pretty well and enjoyed making new sounds on the piano. My mom caught on to this passive interest and threw me into lessons when I was seven, despite my protests. My teacher was a lovely old lady named Sallie Meier, and she taught piano lessons for forty years in her living room. They were dirt cheap, seven dollars for a half-hour, a rate only increasing to eight dollars during the six years that I took lessons from her. She helped me build a classical foundation and taught me how to read music."

While attending middle school, Freiburg participated in various choirs. "I have always loved music, but I don't recall singing as being something I especially enjoyed until I was 11 or 12. I gained confidence in my singing voice by being in choir." At 13, he was introduced to the music of Jerry Lee Lewis: "My choir teacher handed our men's chorus a warm-up piece called 'Great Balls of Fire.' The vocals were certainly fun and wild, but what caught my attention more was the boogie-woogie style that my teacher played on the piano. After class, I asked her about it. She told me his name and said that he was a piano player and singer from the 1950s. Curious, I scoured YouTube that evening. That was the beginning of a serious interest in his piano style, swagger, confidence and speed. I wanted to be able to do that, so I spent hours practicing over the next few months. I can't fathom the number of times I watched his *Steve Allen Show* performance, from 1957." The discovery of Lewis' catalogue opened up a whole new world of possibilities to Freiburg and introduced him to other rock and roll artists.

"At the end of seventh grade, I performed for the first time, to an audience of about 1300 peers. Two of my friends were in the band, and we played 'Great Balls of Fire.' I blush with embarrassment watching the performance these days, but I can remember all too clearly the rush that it gave me and the confidence from the affirmation that the wild audience provided to me. Around that same time, *Million Dollar Quartet* had finished its Broadway run and had come to Des Moines, to the Civic Center. My cousin Stephanie had the idea to take our grandma and me to the show, and it was fantastic. Ben Goddard of the U.K. played Jerry Lee, and I had the chance to speak with him after. He was very nice and encouraging. From that point, an idea grew in the back of my mind that I could someday do that show. Of course, when I was older and had more practice." Freiburg ceased taking piano lessons and instead taught himself: "I preferred to put the book down and play more by ear."

For the next few years, honing his piano skills was his main concentration. Still, he also found time to act in theatrical productions: "I participated in four shows in high school, and then in the winter seasons I was featured in different theater-based ensembles through a program called the Iowa High School Speech Association. That led to many live performances. [Those] experiences helped me work through any type of stage fright I had at the time."

As a senior in 2015, he was chosen to sing in the GRAMMY jazz choir: "Every year, the GRAMMY foundation accepts submissions from U.S. high school students. Of these submissions, they select individuals to fill a jazz band, a jazz quartet and a vocal jazz choir. A very talented friend of mine, Stephanie Hansen, had auditioned and gotten in as a senior. After hearing about the incredible experience she had, I expressed interest in auditioning. Her father, who was a jazz musician, spent hours practicing with me, so I could get a solid audition to send in. They selected me as one of the two tenors for the final group. I was very surprised and very excited to be chosen. Our ensembles were never part of the televised portion, but we had gigs all over L.A. that week and played at the GRAMMY after-party. We sang arrangements from many different artists, such as Ray Charles and The Manhattan Transfer. It was the hardest I had ever worked on anything."

Upon graduation, Freiburg studied jazz performance at the Bob Cole Conservatory of Music at California State University in Long Beach. However, in February 2016, he discovered he was in trouble financially: "Tuition debt seemed to be leading me to drop out and return to Iowa. Then a good friend of mine, Graham Knight, sent me information regarding an open audition for the CMT TV show *Million Dollar Quartet*, later named *Sun Records*. I desperately wanted to try out for the part of Jerry Lee, so I used the rest of my cash to buy a plane ticket to Memphis and then waited in line to perform for members of the production team and, most importantly, Chuck Mead. Chuck was in charge of music for the show, and he was also the music director for

You Sound Just Like...

[the stage show] *Million Dollar Quartet*. They cast somebody else as Jerry Lee for the TV show, but a month later, a different call came up for the Norwegian Cruise Line production of *Million Dollar Quartet*. I drove to that audition, and Chuck advised the casting team to hire me that same day. I then dropped out of college as I needed to appear at rehearsals by the end of that month."

For *Million Dollar Quartet*, Freiburg typically performs to crowds of 300 or less in small theaters: "It is a much more intimate setting and definitely requires a different approach, especially with the acting." Freiburg takes pride in his work and tries hard to enhance his performance by replicating Lewis' signature 1950s hairstyle: "Nobody has hair like Jerry Lee, but in my case, I tend to grow it out to a similar length and tightly comb it back with a fairly large amount of American Crew pomade. Then I add heat with a hairdryer to encourage much of the natural wave my hair already has. The entire process probably takes 25 minutes. In addition to the actual styling, my hair has mild bleaching and highlights throughout its brown base."

One of his most embarrassing moments occurred while he was starring in *Million Dollar Quartet*: "There are things that happen every once in a blue moon, such as power failure, forgotten lyrics or bloody fingers all over the keys, but on one particular night I must have had a little more adrenaline than usual and kicked the piano bench back much higher and further than I was supposed to. The bench left the stage and went straight towards the heads of some audience members. Luckily, the individuals around that section had quick reflexes and blocked the bench from doing any harm. I felt terrible, but they were impressed, rather than angry."

Freiburg also honors Lewis' music in his own stage show, *The Killer Live: A Tribute to Jerry Lee Lewis*. "[When I do a short version,] more attention is focused on the obvious hits, such as 'Great Balls of Fire,' 'Whole Lotta Shakin' Goin' On,' 'Breathless' and 'Crazy Arms.' If there is more time, then I throw in some of my personal favorites: 'Real Wild Child,' 'I'm on Fire,' 'It'll Be Me,' 'You Win Again,' 'Mean Woman Blues,' 'Milkshake Mademoiselle,' 'Chantilly Lace' and 'Hello, Hello Baby.' Jerry Lee could play tons of songs, so there is no end to the stylistic nuances that I continue to uncover through the history of his very long career."

In April 2019, Freiburg recorded an EP consisting of four original tunes and one cover, "Folsom Prison Blues/Mystery Train." He stated, "The title track, 'Vegabond' is a classic rock and roll tune while the others range from shuffle blues to jazz fusion. I wrote 'Vegabond' while I was staying with a good friend of mine, on my way to doing a production in California. It's a song about being away from home often, doing what you can to keep gigging, and being restless in the pursuit of the next adventure." A successful Kickstarter campaign led to the issuance of the EP in June 2019. Freiburg often performs the original material on cruise ships. He dedicates every show to his grandmother, whose faith in him helped him to persevere. However, he has his own dedication to thank for his staying power: "I had to really believe in myself to get to this point, and I wouldn't have had it any other way."

Doug Cooke

For 20 years, Doug Cooke performed as a solo artist at nursing homes and assisted living centers. He recalled, "I met some really sweet people. One of them, Doris, would always tell me, 'You need to write a song.' After hearing that for a while, I finally decided to do so, but not knowing what to write about, I wrote about her. I sang 'Doris' for her whenever I played at her residence. I even printed out the lyrics, so she could have a copy."[4] Incidentally, it's the only song he's ever written. Since 2014, Cooke rarely plays shows locally but has stayed busy with the tribute shows *Killer and the King* and *Cash, Killer, and the King*. In the productions, Cooke portrays Jerry Lee Lewis; Neil Morrow plays Johnny Cash and Scot Bruce is Elvis Presley. Cooke has met and befriended Lewis. In May 2021, Cooke participated in a fundraising event held at the Jerry Lee Lewis Ranch in Nesbit, Mississippi. The Facebook live stream helped raise money for the upkeep of Lewis' home. Cooke performed several of Lewis's hits on his piano.

Cooke didn't begin singing or playing piano with purpose until he was 19, but he remembers singing Neil Diamond's "Song Sung Blue" to his mother when he was only three. His father introduced him to roots music: "I remember sitting on the floor and playing his 45 RPM record collection on our record player. He had Mr. Lewis' 'Whole Lotta Shakin' Goin' On,' but he was mainly into Chuck Berry, Little Richard and Larry Williams. At that time, Sha Na Na had just become popular and had a TV variety show, so I had more '50s music in front of me with that. My dad took my sisters and me to see Sha Na Na in concert at the DC Armory [in Washington, D.C.]. It was my first concert ever."

While in high school, Cooke saw a documentary on the history of rock and roll: "I was trying to be a volleyball player for the Maryland

You Sound Just Like...

Doug Cooke was first exposed to roots music via his dad's 45 RPM record collection: "I remember sitting on the floor and playing them on our record player. He had Jerry Lee Lewis's 'Whole Lotta Shakin' Goin' On,' but he was mostly into Chuck Berry, Little Richard and Larry Williams" (courtesy Doug Cooke).

Three. "It'll Be Me"

State team, so I wasn't yet into music, but I took notice of Jerry Lee Lewis. A few years later, in 1989, the movie *Great Balls of Fire* came out. It had a great soundtrack and some interesting scenes, so I went back two nights later to see it again, and that's when I said, 'I want to do that, right there!' After that, I tried to find out as much as I could about Mr. Lewis and learn the piano." Cooke purchased all the Lewis records and CDs he could find. The more he listened, the bigger fan he became. He added, "[His appeal to me] was a combination of the sound he produced—both on piano and vocally, the casual yet intricate style in which he played, and of course how cool he looked playing the piano." Lewis and his peers are Cooke's main influences, but he listens to all kinds of music, such as Fats Waller, The Bee Gees, Stevie Wonder, Ray Charles, Glenn Miller, Fred Astaire, Moon Mullican, Dale Watson and Bob Wills.

On August 3, 1991, Cooke saw Lewis in concert for the first time at the Rocky Gap Music Festival in Cumberland, Maryland: "It was a blast; I think he was really on point in '91. I first met him in 1996 at the 9:30 Club [in Washington, D.C.]. During the performance, he stopped a song early during the performance and explained his reasoning to the crowd, then turned and pointed to me and said, 'He's a piano player. He knows what I'm talking about.' After the encore, I got backstage to meet him, thanks to my friend and local piano player Daryl Davis. Mr. Lewis' wife Kerrie thought I was venue security and was closing the door on me when Mr. Lewis said, 'Let that guy in. He's a piano player.' As I shook his hand, I asked, 'How did you know that?' He just smiled and went onto a new subject. I'm still delightfully perplexed by that.

Cooke said, "I've probably seen him perform more than 20 times. I've been lucky enough to know him, at least for a spell. In 2000, I was at a piano event in downtown Washington, D.C. where Mr. Lewis was getting an award, and I was introduced to his daughter Phoebe. It was a long event, so there was a lot of time to chat. She and I ended up clicking as pals and stayed in touch. We became good friends, and with her living at the ranch looking after her dad, I ended up seeing both of them quite frequently—to the point that they began to feel like my cousins in Mississippi. He was always kind and never failed to ask how my parents were doing, which I always appreciated. That lasted about ten years, but then the whole dynamic sort of fell apart when Phoebe married, and Mr. Lewis married again. We had a lot of fun times at the ranch."

In 2014, Cooke received a call from Neil Morrow with an offer to perform in the stage show *Cash, Killer, and the King*: "I had known Neil for

You Sound Just Like...

a while, and I told him if he ever needed a backup, I'd be glad to do it. In 2018, I got promoted to the starting role." Morrow stars as Cash; Cooke is Lewis, and Scot Bruce is Presley. "We have a really talented, high-energy band, which I think helps separate us from other competing shows. Our lead guitarist is Travis Daggett. He seamlessly backs all three artists' styles and tones. Jonny Bowler plays bass, and holding down the beat on the drums is Jon Shelley. I have a lot of respect for our band, and I'm really happy I get to play with them." Casinos and theaters in Southern California, Arizona and Nevada showcase the tributes. The venues usually hold 300 to 500 people: "I like the personal connection you can get with a smaller theater, and it can be way more fun." Cooke performs for 20 minutes, then backs the other acts for the remainder of the 90 minutes.

Even though the tribute show is carefully staged, accidents can happen. Cooke mentioned, "Having the possibility of something go wrong is part of the excitement; you do what you can to avoid it, but sometimes it still finds you. I haven't had anything too dreadful occur, but more than once, I have broken the piano stand by making a Jerry Lee move—where I sit on the piano at the end of a song. On one occasion, I flat-out broke the stand, and the piano slammed to the floor. I lucked out, though, as it was the last song in my set, and people thought it was intentional. I also benefitted by my set-closing right before intermission, so then we could get the stand repaired by taping it together. I tried to make the same move on another show more gently, but sure enough, one side of the stand holding up the piano cracked. I was able to catch the piano with one hand before it fell, but I had to play the last song, 'Great Balls of Fire,' with my knee holding up that side of the piano. [Consequently,] I don't sit on piano stands any more."

"Great Balls of Fire" remains one of his favorites to play: "In the show, we build up to it. The song is already a crowd-pleaser, but we leave some room in the arrangement to really crescendo to a big finish. I enjoy the fun of that musical challenge—trying to exceed the audience's expectations of a big hit. 'You Win Again' is another favorite of mine to play. I love Mr. Lewis' Sun Records version. I'm really impressed that he came up with that tasty arrangement at 21, and it showed that he played a lot in church."

An album was prepared to aid in the promotion of *Cash, Killer and the King*: "It was recorded in Moreno Valley, California, with Travis Daggett producing. He stuck some microphones into a banged-up spinet piano, and we took it from there. I tried to include some songs that I like—deeper tracks in his catalogue. We had a lot of fun making

Three. "It'll Be Me"

it." In the lobby of each venue, audience members can purchase a copy of the album and speak with the tribute artists. Cooke said, "I enjoy meeting the folks who come to the shows. One guy told me he saw Jerry Lee and Chuck Berry on Alan Freed's *Big Beat* show back in the '50s. I was excited to hear a first-person account of that."

Jacob Tolliver

Dick Van Dyke, Tony Bennett and Jerry Lee Lewis are the artists that really sparked a flame inside Jacob Tolliver to want to get into show biz. They are his top three influences.

Portraying Lewis has been Tolliver's claim to fame, and it all started a month before he would have embarked on a college education at Ohio State University. For the next four years, he starred as Lewis in

Jacob Tolliver (left) and Jerry Lee Lewis have developed a tight-knit friendship. Tolliver has toured with Lewis, has given tours of Lewis's home, and even performed at Lewis's 85th birthday party. He considers Lewis part of his family (courtesy Jacob Tolliver).

You Sound Just Like...

the musical *Million Dollar Quartet*. In 2015, he auditioned for *American Idol* in Minneapolis. He sang "Whole Lotta Shakin' Goin' On." Unfortunately, one of the judges, Keith Urban, felt Tolliver was great at mimicking Lewis but not representing himself, so Urban asked for another song. "Stay with Me" by Sam Smith was Tolliver's choice. He then qualified for the next round. Tolliver made it to Hollywood Week before being eliminated.

These days, original music is at the forefront of Tolliver's mind, and he has aspirations to release an album. In 2018, he duetted with *Full House* alum Jodie Sweetin on the holiday classic "Santa Baby." Ironically, before its release, the song was Tolliver's least favorite Christmas tune. That same year, he was the opening act for Lewis on 20 shows.

Tolliver was born on November 17, 1993, in Portsmouth, Ohio. He revealed, "When my parents would be at work, my grandmother would watch me, and she always had her radio on in the kitchen, [tuned to] an oldies station. I think I just subconsciously absorbed all of those songs that were being played. When I got a little older, my grandmother and I would go to a local antique shop. They had a huge record collection, so I would go through and pick out records each week and then come home with "new" vinyl. I started chronologically going through time, as far as music goes. I liked Bing Crosby, The Andrews Sisters, Glenn Miller and his Orchestra and The Boswell Sisters. When I was seven, Elvis Presley was the newest artist I liked. I slowly got into The Rolling Stones, AC/DC, etc."[5] Regarding singing, Tolliver can't remember a time when he didn't: "*Elvis—in Person at the International Hotel, Las Vegas, Nevada*, was the first Elvis CD I ever got. I remember specifically trying to memorize all the words to those songs, so my first song was probably 'Blue Suede Shoes' or 'Hound Dog,' maybe 'Johnny B. Goode.'"

At the age of nine, while in the third grade, Tolliver took piano lessons: "My parents and grandmother wanted to put me through them, so I took lessons for nine months, but I did horribly. My piano teacher was very prim and proper, a great lady, but we were just not a fit because I was using my ear to play, and she was reading the notes on a page. I would slowly read the page once, and then I would memorize it after that and then just start playing by ear. The next week when I went to my lesson, I would jazz it up, and of course, she was reading along with the page and would catch me. She went to my parents and said, 'Look, he's a lost cause. He's not trying to learn. He's not trying to read music.' My parents pulled me out of the lessons, and I was fine with that [decision] because I did not like it."

Three. "It'll Be Me"

Tolliver acknowledged, "I kept telling everybody, 'I want to play the fun stuff.' I didn't know what that meant, but I knew that I was not doing it. I was doing scales and basic stuff, and that just did not interest me at all. I was so tired and fed up with playing the piano that way, so I quit for three years. [One day,] I was cleaning my bedroom and from under my bed. My keyboard was under there, so I pulled it out, dusted it off and plugged it in. I started playing a boogie-woogie bassline. My dad was walking through the house and said, 'Was that you?' I said, 'Yeah.' He said, 'Well, don't stop that,' so I kept playing. When I was at school, I would make every excuse I could to go to the music room to sit at the piano and play. When I was home, I would be at my keyboard. I would also go to my neighbor's and play their piano. I was piano-hopping. You just couldn't keep me off of it now that I was playing by ear and playing stuff that I wanted. I pretty much learned everything in about three months. I understood the keyboard fully at that point."

He commented, "My dad kept saying, 'You need to listen to some Jerry Lee Lewis.' I'm thinking, 'Yeah, yeah, yeah, whatever.' At that age, parents are always wrong, so I would just kind of roll my eyes and say, 'Sure, dad.' Finally, about six months later, he called the radio station one night and requested that they play 'Great Balls of Fire.' It came on the radio about 45 minutes later, and my mind was blown because that was exactly the style that I was doing. I was certainly a fan the moment I heard Jerry. It was amazing, and I went out the next day and got a Jerry Lee Lewis cassette. From there, I started listening to Little Richard and Fats Domino, then Elton John and Leon Russell, all the piano greats." The first song Tolliver played was "Johnny B. Goode."

In high school, Tolliver impressed his teachers and fellow students with his boogie-woogie piano stylings: "A friend of mine was interested in videography, so he was always recording and putting stuff up on YouTube. He would offer to record me playing piano in our school choir room. After school or during our lunch period, we would record a song." In one clip, Tolliver plays a Little Richard tune.

"I was working at a local pizza and ice cream shop, and when I got home that night, I checked my email. I had a notification from YouTube saying that somebody had commented on my [Little Richard] video. It read, 'Hey, we are Adorama Casting in Las Vegas. Please give us a call at this number.' I called them the next day, and they said, 'We want to fly you out tomorrow for an audition.' Of course, I was super-excited, but I said, 'Whoa, can I talk to my parents first about this?' My parents were completely shocked because it was 100 percent out of the blue. I was a

You Sound Just Like...

month away from going to Ohio State. Everything was paid for. My parents and I talked about it that night. I called the [casting company] back right away and said, 'My parents say, "Let's do it."' We figured it wouldn't hurt to audition." The tryout landed Tolliver the role of Lewis in the musical *Million Dollar Quartet* at Harrah's Casino in Las Vegas. For the first two years or so, he was the understudy. The stint overall lasted for four years.

His most embarrassing moment occurred while starring in *Million Dollar Quartet*: "The show had gone perfectly that night. Everybody was firing on all cylinders. It was a sold-out crowd, and the audience was great. We were doing the finale song, 'See You Later, Alligator,' and I'm sitting at the piano, on the edge of the bench, just rockin' out. I was about to take a piano solo when, all of a sudden, the bench flips out from under me. Before I know it, my hands are above my head playing the piano, and my butt is sitting on the floor." Despite his shock, Tolliver kept performing.

Those shows were high-energy, so he and the rest of the cast couldn't just leave the stage, go home and go straight to sleep. Instead, they would venture to a local Las Vegas restaurant called The Peppermill: "We'd chill there for a couple of hours, just talk, eat and have fun. That was kind of our way of getting back down to Earth."

These days, Tolliver concentrates on making a mark with his own shows: "Sometimes, it's a three-hour show and sometimes it's 15 minutes, just depends on what the person booking me wants. I mix everything [into my sets]. I throw in a couple of Jerry Lee songs, some original music, covers by Lady Gaga, Queen, The Rolling Stones, etc. For some reason, and I don't know why, a personal favorite for me to play has always been 'Drinkin' Wine Spo-Dee-O-Dee.' It's simple and easy, but there's something fun about it. I also get a kick out of playing 'That Lucky Old Sun.'" As far as recording, he has been working on original songs: "I've been going to Nashville for the past few years, and I've been collaborating with Rick Ferrell." Ferrell wrote the #1 hit "Something Like That" for Tim McGraw and the #3 hit "Where Would You Be" for Martina McBride. "He's a brilliant lyricist, and I'm not at all. Rick and I have been slowly fine-tuning my sound and have finally gotten the vibe of the songs. We are almost to the point where we can go into the studio and record."

In 2018, Tolliver collaborated with actress Jodie Sweetin on the Christmas single release "Santa Baby." He admitted, "Growing up in the '90s, I watched *Full House* [which Sweetin is known for], and I enjoyed

Three. "It'll Be Me"

it when I saw it. I met Jodie because Jeff Franklin, the creator of *Full House*, throws crazy, outlandish Hollywood dinner parties, and through a mutual friend, I got invited to his house one night." Usually the entire *Full House* cast was in attendance, and after dinner, everybody would move into the living room and a jam session would begin. Tolliver recalled, "Once I played piano and did duets all night with Tom Jones."

The Beach Boys and The Rolling Stones have also shown up: "Mick Jagger instantly recognized me from my viral hardware store video of 'Whole Lotta Shakin' Goin' On.' It was so surreal! It stopped me in my tracks for a second. He was extremely gracious and overall a true gentleman. A moment I'll never forget."[6] Incidentally, Jagger, Tom Jones and Tony Bennett are his favorite singers. Tolliver remembered, "At some point, at one of these parties, Jodie expressed an interest in singing. She would do a couple of songs by herself, and then we just decided to start playing around and performing together. We did 'Jackson' and songs like that. We did that for six months to a year, and finally we said, 'You know what, we're having fun with it, and people enjoy it. Why not actually record something?'" Soon after, "Santa Baby" was born.

Tolliver's life changed when he befriended Jerry Lee Lewis and his wife Judith: "I first met them in 2013. I had a video of me playing 'Whole Lotta Shakin' Goin' On' in a hardware store that went viral on Facebook. People kept sharing this video with Judith's Facebook page, so she finally friended me and reached out. She just said, 'Hey, darling, I want to let you know that the Killer and I think you're great. Anything we can do to help, let us know.' We then kept in touch. She invited me to visit the next time I was in Memphis. My dad and I went and hung out with them [at their house] for a couple of hours. We just talked." For two years, Tolliver opened for Lewis. The first time was at a casino in Minnesota. "When we were on the road, he would have the monitor on in the dressing room, and he'd listen to my show. He always had some commentary, usually positive, which was relieving because having Jerry listen to your show is very daunting. He was specific, such as saying, 'I like how you had that break in the middle of the song, and then you went into a faster tempo,' or, 'I like how you started off with this song and then went into a completely different one.' If I did a slow country song, he would [joke] and say, 'Well, killer, I think you oughta stick to rock and roll.' We've really bonded. I love him and his wife to death. I'd do anything for them. It's an awesome relationship."

Four

Pop–Rock and Roll Icons

Al Jackson (Fats Domino)

Fats Domino is one of the architects of rock and roll, and Al Jackson feels a great responsibility to honor him properly: "Being 'Lil Fats' is a lot of fun but also physically and emotionally exhausting. He is so out-of-character for me that it's like walking a tightrope for hours."[1] Nevertheless, Jackson has succeeded in giving an uncanny representation, from his vocals to his appearance: "Fats Domino fans, when they first see and hear me, wonder if it's real or some kind of trick. A lady once grabbed the mike I was singing into to see if the vocal would continue."

In truth, Jackson naturally sounds like Domino: "I have always spoken the way I do. When I was a little boy, people used to call me 'Old Man,' because of it. The people I looked up to, in my formative years, shaped me. If you had ever heard them

When Al Jackson's mother insisted that he perform a few songs at her Christmas work party, he was crippled with anxiety. But if he refused, her car would be off-limits for the weekend, so he relented. He played three songs from the Fats Domino album *Christmas Is a Special Day* and his mother's favorite Domino tune, "Oh What a Price." He was a big hit (courtesy Al Jackson).

Four. Pop–Rock and Roll Icons

speak and Fats speak, you'd understand. You take French-Creole accents and add New Orleans notes, and you've got Fats Domino but also Al Jackson." Besides wowing audiences, he also made a fan out of Domino: "I performed the night his statue was unveiled in the French Quarter. I wasn't able to talk to him that night but later he said I was good." These days, Jackson and his seven-piece band stay busy playing to sold-out crowds at casinos, fairs, and festivals throughout the country.

Jackson was born on December 28, 1973, in Marrero, Louisiana. He revealed, "When I was a little boy, I spent a lot of time with my grandfather. I would get up really early in the morning, and we would talk. He would tell me stories before he went to work. When he got home, we'd watch cartoons and westerns together. The most fun was had when he shared his record collection with me. My great grandmother owned a nightclub called the Vet's Club in Bridge City, Louisiana, and my grandfather kept the 45 RPM records from the jukebox. He had a huge collection, which included Smiley Lewis, Tommy Ridgley, Huey 'Piano' Smith, Ernie K-Doe, but Fats Domino was the artist who most excited me. He could sing the blues and make you feel happy about it."

Jackson added, "I've always loved Fats Domino's music. There are many reasons why, but I believe the number one draw was his delivery of the lyrics. Now when I hear Fats, it reminds me of my grandparents and some very happy times. My grandfather, John Hill, was my biggest fan, greatest friend, and most valuable asset on the road."

At six years old, Jackson sang his first song, the B.B. King blues tune "Never Make Your Move Too Soon." "I used to pretend to play [piano] on the back of a striped sofa in my grandparents' den while I listened to my uncle's record player. When I was ten, my Aunt Elenore's boyfriend left a tiny Casio keyboard-calculator at our house. It only had buttons, not keys, but I loved it. A couple of years later, he came back and took it. It hit me so hard that my mom went out and bought me one of my own. This one was bigger, and I really took to it. I started to pick out melodies and figure out chords. It was great. However, I was stuck for a very long time trying to figure out 'Blueberry Hill.' It drove me crazy.

"Then one night as I fell asleep, I began to dream about piano keys. First there was just silence and then the keys. I could hear someone putting the needle on a record and saw a hand appearing over the keys and just as 'Blueberry Hill' began to play, the hand played the song on the keys. I was so excited that I sprung out of my bed and went right to the keyboard and played 'Blueberry Hill' for the first time. I didn't realize it was 3 a.m., so I was shocked when my mother threatened to throw me and my keyboard out my bedroom window." It wasn't until Jackson was in high school that he played an actual piano: "My mom thought it was a good idea to have me take piano lessons from a lady named Mrs. Tillman. She taught me a few basics, but what she wanted to play I didn't like, and she didn't like what I added to some of the pieces, so that didn't last long."

Jackson acknowledged, "My mom has a very strong personality and usually gets her way. She is the reason I got my first public event. I was 19 and just home from college. My mother, having heard me mess around with the keyboard and sing for years, wanted me to play a few songs at her Christmas work party. She was a deputy in the New Orleans criminal court at Tulane and Broad Street, and Judge Jerome Winsberg was throwing the party. (He was also a Fats fan.) My mother thought it was a great idea to have me play at this party. You must understand that this was a complete nightmare for me. Introvert doesn't say enough about my personality. The idea of going in front of non–family members and singing was so crazy, I thought she was joking. She was not. Up until five minutes before I had to leave, I was frozen with fear and anxiety. I finally went because I did not have my own car, and if I hadn't [cooperated], then my mother's car would be off limits for the weekend. [On a battery-powered keyboard,] I played three songs from the Fats album *Christmas Is a Special Day* and my mother's favorite, 'Oh What a Price.' The judge was very happy, but I just wanted to go. Everyone enjoyed it, but there was one person who seemed to not want me there. He sat on a couch directly in front of me, staring at me the whole time with his arms folded. [When I tried to leave,] he blocked my exit. Introducing himself as Joe Cardinia, he wanted to be my agent if I was willing to 'do this for money.' This was another time when I thought someone was joking, but he was not. I worked my second private party the following Saturday." The pay was $60.

Initially, Jackson didn't have his own band, so he would sit in with various groups. His most memorable appearance occurred at My Father's Junk Yard on 4th Street in Marrero: "At the time, I hadn't shortened my name, and for some reason, maybe my accent, instead of Alvin Jackson, people heard Alan Jackson. For an entire month, there was a flyer going around that advertised 'Alan Jackson: Live at the Junk Yard.' I didn't realize this until I arrived [at the venue] because my grandfather had pointed it out to me. The place was packed, all expecting to see Alan Jackson. Considering the fact that this club was well-stocked with country music lovers, you can imagine my terror. The time came; the introduction was made—'Ladies and gentlemen, Alan Jackson.' There was crazy applause but then when I walked out on stage—a skinny black kid wearing a blue suit with a bald fade haircut—there was dead silence. I then sat down at the keyboard (absolutely terrified), but the guitar player said, 'Just start, it'll be all right.' I did, and by the time I was five songs in, I had them reeling and rocking."

A short time later, Frankie and Johnny's, a local furniture store, commissioned Jackson to write and perform a jingle for one of their TV ads. Fats Domino saw the commercial. In early 1997, their paths crossed, "I was working at a fundraiser for a local judge, and just before my set ended, a local New Orleans legend named Oliver 'Who Shot the LaLa' Morgan came in. He came up to me when I was done and said, 'More people need to know about you. I'm going to take you around with me.' He then asked if I had ever met Fats Domino since I'd been doing his music for a living. I said no. He told me that he would bring me to his house and make the introduction. I didn't believe it, but less than a week later I received a phone call from Oliver. He said he wanted me to meet him at his house in the 9th Ward of New Orleans, and he would drive me over to meet Fats. I still didn't believe it until we were standing at Fats' front door. After a knock, there he was. Oliver introduced me, and before he was done, Fats reached for my hand, grabbed it, leaned in and sang 'See the special man,' which was the hook line for the jingle I wrote for the Frankie and Johnny's furniture store.

"If, at that moment, he had said goodbye and slammed the door, I would still have counted it among the greatest moments of my life, but as I learned in years to come, Fats was all about hospitality. He invited us in and gave us a tour of his house. He and Oliver talked about stuff as if nothing all that special was happening, but I was losing my mind. Just as I was finally gaining a little composure, we got to his piano. He pointed to it and said, 'Let me see what you got.' I've re-told this time and time again, and every time I do, I get goosebumps. Anyway, I sat at his piano, and I drew a complete blank. I know hundreds of Fats songs, and I couldn't think of one to play. After what seemed like an eternity of silence, Oliver said, 'Play "The Fat Man."' This is my favorite song, but one of the most difficult for me to play. Many people call it a rock and roll song, but it's really more barrel-house than rock. It has a lot going on in it. I plunged into it, and Fats stood there listening, then said, 'You almost got it, but let me show you.' Then a master sat next to me and played one of his masterpieces. I watched and listened, and I hope one day to play it like he did. I get close."

You Sound Just Like...

Jackson commented, "That first day, he gave me some advice. He said, 'In all things, put God first.' I'd heard this all my life from my parents, and the truth is, it has never left me."

Eventually, Jackson and his grandfather befriended Domino: "We were able to pick up the phone, call him, and actually have him answer. That was a true honor and privilege. I saw Fats many, many times live, but one time will always be the best. It was the grand opening of Harrah's Casino in New Orleans; Fats performed on the riverfront that night. He had asked if my grandpa and I would be there. I wasn't certain because we would be coming in from Houston and didn't know if we would make it in time. He had passes waiting for us, and we got there during his first song. I walked to the front of the stage and after he was done, he looked over and saw me standing there. He said through his mike, 'Hey, "Lil' Al!"' Then he got up from his piano, walked to the edge of the stage, reached down, and shook my hand. There are photos floating around out there somewhere of that very moment. Sadly, I lost my copy in Hurricane Katrina."

Domino's friend and recording partner, Dave Bartholomew, was also intrigued by Jackson's portrayal: "One night, while playing at Boomtown New Orleans Casino in Harvey, Louisiana, I saw a man standing at the entrance. His silhouette caught my attention for some reason, and I asked my grandfather to go and ask the man who he was. He came back to the stage and said, 'That was Dave Bartholomew.' When Dave first walked up, I was doing 'I Hear You Knockin'.' My grandfather said it grabbed Dave's attention because he wrote that song, and I was doing it right. I didn't get a chance to meet him that night, but in 2015, I did, when I co-starred in the play *Walking to New Orleans*, which was about Fats and Dave's [musical] partnership. He was a fountain of knowledge [regarding the] business end of the recording industry."

Louisiana is Jackson's home base, so he regularly plays its casinos—Boomtown New Orleans Casino in Harvey; Treasure Chest Casino in Kenner, and Cypress Bayou Casino in Charenton. He is also a big hit at the Silver Slipper Casino in Bay St. Louis, Mississippi. He drew his largest audience when he was musical guest on the Grand Marshal float in the Endymion Parade: "We got to Canal Street, and I felt like I was on a boat floating in a sea of people. There were thousands. It was so loud and crazy.

"Typically, my performances are about an hour and 15 minutes, but sometimes I get caught up in [honoring] requests and I lose track of time. I don't normally play from a song list. My show is called a tribute act by many, and that is apt, but it's never been only Fats Domino songs. It includes music from artists that he influenced and also from those who influenced him: Lloyd Price, Smiley Lewis, Dave Bartholomew, Chubby Checker, Clarence 'Frogman' Henry, Chris Kenner and many others. I choose certain well-known songs to kinda test the audience's mood. 'Blue Monday' and 'Blueberry Hill' are staples, and they tell me if the audience has come to listen or to dance. From there, I just follow the flow. Incidentally, 'The Fat Man' has always been my favorite song to perform because it's unique among his works, and it was his first. His early tunes have much more piano work in them, so I guess that's why I like them best."

Jesse Aron (Roy Orbison)

Nicknamed "The Voice," Jesse Aron was contacted by Roy Orbison's longtime guitarist and manager, Alan James Painter, to headline tours with him. This has become a yearly tradition since it began in 2018. His Orbison tribute has gained in popularity, rivaling his homage to the King of Rock and Roll. Life as an Elvis Tribute Artist began in 1997. Since then, he has won multiple championships, including first place at both the 2009 Images of the King and the 2013 Collingwood Elvis Festival.

Aron was born on September 16, 1975, in Chicago, Illinois. At age two, he began singing. His first tune was "Heartbreak Hotel," which he pronounced as "Breakheart Hotel." He stated, "Through my parents, I was drawn to Elvis. They had a rock and roll band, and the rehearsals were in my house in Chicago."[2] His father also did a tribute to Presley. In fact, Aron used to run off with his father's records, so he could practice in front of his bedroom mirror. One of the songs was "Hurt," which he performed over and over because it was so challenging. At that time, he was too shy to showcase his talent in front of anyone.

Aron's first performance was a lip sync contest at his high school; sporting his father's jumpsuit, he won third place. In 1997, he participated in an open mike night held at an Edgerton, Wisconsin, restaurant and decided to enter the world of Elvis Tribute Artists. Aron then performed at local fairs and nightclubs in and around Janesville, Wisconsin. Prior to this, he had worked in a warehouse and occasionally impersonated Michael Jackson.

In January 2003, he competed in his first Elvis Tribute Artist

You Sound Just Like…

A lifelong fan of both Halloween and Roy Orbison, Jesse Aron introduced the music of Orbison to the crowd one year at his Halloween show. It was a huge hit, and he's been paying tribute to Orbison ever since (courtesy Jesse Aron).

contest, held at the Potawatomi Casino in Milwaukee. He took home the prize, $10,000. He recalled, "I had gotten so scared that I made myself sick and lost my voice." Fortunately for him, the audience response got him through. "It was nerve-wracking, but the outcome was amazing."[3] He still regularly participates in competitions; performances at theaters, casinos, and festivals occupy the rest of his schedule. Crowd size has varied from 50 to 30,000. "I'm constantly preparing and rehearsing, always learning something new. The best prep is rehearsal—not live or online, but privately in my home studio. I have to connect to the songs, so whatever mood I'm in dictates my favorite."

His Roy Orbison tribute started when he decided to incorporate a new act into his annual Halloween show: "I tried it out, and people loved it." Orbison is one of his favorite singers along with Presley, Jackie Wilson, Ricky Nelson and Michael Bublé. In February 2018, Alan James Painter, Orbison's former guitarist and manager, discovered Aron online and was so impressed by his talent that he contacted him. He requested that Aron headline a tour of Florida with him in a show called *Forever Orbison*. Aron happily agreed, and this tradition has continued every spring. Painter has credited Aron with bringing his friend back.

Aron's wife Tarie used to perform alongside him with her impersonations of Marilyn Monroe and Connie Francis; now that she's retired from entertaining, he hires other ladies to work with him on his tours. Aron acknowledged, "I am just a tribute artist, and I enjoy that very much." He added, "The best part of being an ETA is making people happy by forgetting about reality for a while and taking them to another place ... just the happiness and laughs it brings them."[4]

Rick Lindy (Roy Orbison)

Rick Lindy is another of those artists who isn't an impersonator, but rather an interpreter of songs: "My tributes are salutes to the artists. I would never dye my hair or put on a wig."[5] His career began with a two-year stint in The Serendipity Singers. After that, he starred in a series of bands. Lately, Lindy has found success playing hundreds of dates out of a calendar year with his band the Wild Ones. He has also opened for some of the biggest names in the music business, notably Johnny Cash, Wanda Jackson and Hank Thompson.

Lindy's parents were both musicians and encouraged his endeavors. He acknowledged, "I have been singing since I was old enough to talk. I started on piano at age eight but already had learned how to play some songs by ear. It was a natural talent my father Richard also had. Then, the organ came at age ten and finally guitar at 11. My sister Caren bought me my first guitar. I had a few lessons but mostly self-taught." At seven years of age, Lindy had embarrassed that same sister: "While at her graduation from nursing school, I got on the stage before the commencement and began dancing and singing for the crowd." That was his introduction to a live audience. His musical influences and favorite artists are Marty Robbins, Roy Orbison, Elvis Presley, Hank Williams Sr., Hank Williams Jr., and Patsy Cline. However, "Hank Williams Sr. and Johnny Cash paved the way for my interests." Theater beckoned in high school and that interest continued into college: "I honed my skills and got over stage fright by being in plays." Later, he also participated in Community Theater. Some of the plays in which he has been featured: *The Music Man, How to Succeed in Business Without Really Trying, South Pacific* and *Bye Bye Birdie.*

Rick Lindy named his band the Wild Ones after the Marlon Brando film *The Wild One*. Promoters didn't know the reference and thought that they were a heavy metal band. Overall, that hasn't hurt Lindy's performance schedule as he gets booked for at least 300 dates a year (photograph by Tim Johnson; courtesy Rick Lindy).

In 1990, Lindy became a member of The Serendipity Singers: "After I graduated from the American Academy of Art in Chicago, I was going to join the Marine Corps. Since our country was at war with Iraq in Operation Desert Storm, I felt it was my patriotic duty. My mom didn't want me to go to war. She saw this ad for a traveling singer and guitar player, so I called. I auditioned at a hotel in Schaumburg, Illinois, for the owner John Ross and his mother Jacque. One of the songs I sang was 'Don't Worry' by Marty Robbins." That gig—which didn't pay that well—lasted for two years before he got homesick.

However, while on the road with The Serendipity Singers, he met Johnny Cash: "I was wandering around Washington, D.C., seeing the sights when I came across a music store. In front of that store was a tour bus and over the windshield was a plain sign that said 'Johnny Cash.' I figured Johnny or June could be in the store, and I was correct as Johnny was in there talking to a store employee about a guitar. I went up to him. He saw I had on a Sun Records t-shirt and that I was sporting sideburns and a [coifed] hairstyle. He said, 'Oh, you must be a rockabilly.' I said, 'Yes, sir. You've been a big influence on my music career.' He smiled and extended his hand. The store worker gave me a dirty look, and I could tell he wanted me to go away."

Lindy added, "A few years later, I had the opportunity to open a show for Johnny, so I asked to see him in the green room. The staff agreed and knocked on his door. He said 'Come in,' and as soon as he saw me, he said, 'Well, you have come a long way since Washington, D.C.' He remembered me, and I was pretty thrilled."

That same year, 1990, Lindy made a name for himself as a solo act with the 45 RPM record release "Working Man Blues" backed with "Tantalize My Heart," which was recorded in Nashville for K-Ark Records. Elvis Presley's drummer D.J. Fontana played on the recordings: "It happened by fate. We were talking on the sofa in the lounge of the studio, called Soundtracks. It was the same studio that Willie Nelson cut 'Stardust.' D.J. was next to me and at first I didn't know it was him. He had on a red satin jacket, tinted glasses, and was wearing a horseshoe ring with diamonds. It was when I saw that ring that it clicked, on who he was. D.J. was [then] a session player for the label. My buddy Dave Schrader, who was also my first manager, arranged it."

On October 2, 1992, Lindy and his band, the Cyclones, were hired to open the show and back Hayden Thompson at the Beat Kitchen in Chicago. Also on the bill: Ronnie Dawson and a local act, The Moon Dogs, featuring bassist Jimmy Sutton. Sutton had been a classmate and friend of Lindy's at the American Academy of Art: "Jimmy introduced me to many new avenues of rockabilly." Lindy had befriended Thompson after he had seen that he lived in the Chicago suburbs: "I looked his name up in the phone book, and it said H. Thompson. I called it, and a Southern gentleman answered, who was indeed Hayden. That evening, he was performing at the Cubby Bear in Chicago, and he invited me." Years later, Lindy covered a version of Thompson's Sun record "Love My

You Sound Just Like...

Baby," but this time it was sung as a duet: "I had asked him to guest on it. He didn't ask for any money, but in nearly every conversation [we've had since], he kids me about a royalty check. He had a hit song in the early 1960s called '$16.88.' It's about a guy wanting to ride a train, and the fare is $16.88. As a joke, I mailed him a check for that amount. We still typically speak a few times a year, usually every Christmas Eve he'll call me."

The band Big Guitars from Memphis hired Lindy as their lead singer in 1996. He stayed with them until the early 2000s. During that time, they issued three CDs with original material. In 1999, Lindy formed the Wild Ones, the band he still plays with today: "Todd Menke is the longest running member; we've been playing together since 1992. Other members are Greg Nash, Bart Alonzo, Andy Trippi, Tracy Shepherd, Jim Nelson and Gordon Patriarca. On occasion, Jim Johnson joins us on sax and keys." The band's name pays homage to Marlon Brando's movie *The Wild One*. In 2001 and 2002, Flipside Amigo Records issued two CDs of theirs; they feature all original Lindy compositions. Lindy noted, "I began making up songs and melodies as a child. The process sometimes develops from original poems or sometimes a melody just comes to me. Then I write the lyrics. My songs come from both true experiences and fictional [tales] much like an author who creates a story."

The pandemic quarantined Americans for three months in the spring of 2020. All businesses were closed, except for those that were deemed essential. During that time and for months that followed, many musicians were unable to find work because venues were closed. Lindy suffered the same fate, but he managed to persevere thanks to livestreamed concerts via the internet and merchandise sales. By early 2021, he was again booking gigs. Lindy plays a lot of car shows, restaurants and private events: "The show is based on the client's needs. They range from 45 minutes to four hours. Some songs are originals; some have really touched me emotionally, while others are popular tunes that people expect to hear at a '50s-'60s show. At times, we get requests for songs we don't know. We try to be polite when we cannot do them. On occasion, we give it the old college try and can usually do a pretty good rendition of the unrehearsed song. In the case of my Roy Orbison show, Angelo Sorce [originally] suggested it. However, Roy's songs have always been in my repertoire, so I put it together. It was well received, and bookings have been coming in as a result." His favorite Orbison tunes to sing are "In Dreams" and "The Crowd": "Both are powerful, and I'm happy to be able to sing his material, which is difficult for most."

Besides being a popular act in the Chicagoland area, Lindy has toured Europe numerous times. He stated, "They love rockabilly and roots rock, even more than Americans." On a couple of tours in Denmark and Sweden, Lindy shared a bill with Wanda Jackson, and he opened a show for Hank Thompson in Malmö, Sweden. In 1998, while Lindy was still with his group Big Guitars from Memphis, they played with Robert Gordon at a blues fest in Molde, Norway, and at the Mars Club in Oslo, Norway. Lindy recalled, "Robert was one of my singing idols. I traveled for hours in the car with him. At first, he was quiet and reserved, but as the miles went on, he opened up and gave me his home phone number. I called it twice, and he was kind to me each time."

When Lindy isn't performing, he enjoys watching movies from the 1930s and 1940s with his wife Karen. Some of his favorite actors are Edward G. Robinson, James Cagney, Humphrey Bogart, Marlene Dietrich, Clark Gable and Errol Flynn. He's also a big fan of The Three Stooges. In recent years, Lindy has built a recording studio in his home, which has given him the opportunity to release several CDs. Through his music, he gets the chance to touch people's hearts.

Garry Moore (Little Richard)

Little Richard was known for his flamboyant style and attitude, and Garry Moore stays true to that in his portrayal of the iconic rock and roller. Moore stated, "You want to stay on course with it. Don't let your own personality slip into it."[6] He even incorporates Little Richard's famous "Shut Up!" into his shows. However, the vocals are the hardest to replicate, so Moore usually doesn't play the piano and sing at the same time: "I am not a piano player. I can play a little. I tried taking lessons and practicing, but I am just uncoordinated. Therefore, I just focus on the singing. The vocals are the most important thing to me."[7] Little Richard gave him his stamp of approval, according to Moore: "I first saw him in Laughlin, Nevada, in the mid–1990s. I was working for *Legends in Concert* at Imperial Palace in Las Vegas and had a day off, so I drove to Laughlin to see his show. I then had the opportunity to meet him backstage in his dressing room. I saw him numerous times after that, and I remember the one thing he said when he heard me was, 'You can sing! Call me any time.' That was one of the greatest moments in my career."

Moore began singing with friends in high school. His early musical influences were Elvis Presley, The Beatles, The Rolling Stones, Motown

You Sound Just Like...

artists and Tom Jones. In the 1970s, the list expanded to include Earth, Wind and Fire and Michael Jackson. Moore received a bachelor's degree in communications from the University of Hawaii. His education and seven years of Army service taught him how to communicate with and perform for a live audience. Moore didn't sing in the armed forces, but worked in the Communications Maintenance field as a signal corporate officer. He rose to the rank of captain. In 1990, he took the stage as Little Richard for the first time: "My friend Tony Roi, an Elvis impersonator, convinced me to perform with him on the Jerry Lewis Muscular Dystrophy Telethon. I really did not want to do the telethon, but it was for charity, to help Jerry's kids, so I agreed. I practiced for about a month; it took me many, many hours trying to capture his voice, and Tony helped with the makeup and hair." Moore wore an off-white jacket adorned with rhinestones and sang "Tutti Frutti" and "Lucille." "Tony was the one who said I looked like Little Richard, and I told him 'Shut up!'" At this time, Moore paid tribute to the younger version of Little Richard: "I had the big pompadour for 20 years. It took me an hour to get ready. My routine was brush, comb up, and hold, then spray with Aqua Net and blow dry. It was a pain in the butt. I decided to have the longer hair after doing a TV show, *The Next Best Thing: Who Is the Greatest Celebrity Impersonator?*"

A short lived 2007 series, *The Next Best Thing* was a competition where the winner was awarded $100,000. Moore placed in the Top Ten, but ultimately Elvis Tribute Artist Trent Carlini was crowned champion. During the finale, Moore shared the stage with

One of the greatest moments in Garry Moore's career was when Little Richard told him, "You can sing!" Moore admitted that it wasn't easy to sing like Little Richard (courtesy Garry Moore).

Little Richard. Afterward, they sat backstage and chatted: "We talked about God, religion a little bit, but we talked mostly about how hard it was to sing like him."[8]

From 1993 to 1999, Moore had a steady gig with *Legends in Concert:* "I had auditioned for the original producer, John Stuart, in Atlantic City in 1991. The concept of the show allowed you to do roughly 10 to 15 minutes, so I sang 'Lucille,' 'Good Golly Miss Molly,' 'Jenny, Jenny' and 'Tutti Frutti.' I started with them when they opened the show in Hawaii. It was my home, so it made sense for me to be a part of it in Waikiki. I also worked with them in Las Vegas; Branson, Missouri; Daytona Beach, Florida, and Myrtle Beach, South Carolina, for three months to six months at a time. Wherever I went with the show, the production was at its highest level. *Legends in Concert* was the show to be in. I haven't worked with them for four years now. They changed their direction after it went corporate." Once *Legends in Concert* closed their show in Hawaii in 1999, Moore worked on a cruise ship where he portrayed both Little Richard and Sammy Davis Jr. "Sammy was more of a singer, so it was practice, practice and more practice. I really love trying to sing like him, but I have more fun performing as Little Richard."

As for Little Richard, Moore's favorites to sing are "Lucille," "Good Golly Miss Molly" and "Tutti Frutti." He enjoys incorporating medleys into short sets because then he can squeeze seven songs into ten minutes. His tribute act is hired by theaters, convention centers and large clubs. Within his 45-minute shows, he features songs by a wide range of artists, including Chuck Berry, The Beatles, James Brown and Fats Domino. Performing for charity organizations is also near and dear to Moore's heart. He added, "I even opened for Bruno Mars when he was in his father's band at the Blaisdell Arena in Honolulu, Hawaii, for 8000 people. My biggest audience was where I sang in front of 25,000 people at a University of Hawaii football game."

Moore still performs as Little Richard, but when he's at home in Hawaii, he makes time for his band, Wasabi. In those shows, he sings tunes by Huey Lewis, The Beatles, Elvis and Aerosmith. "As long as I can put a smile on the faces of the people that I perform for and feel the love from at least one individual that appreciates what I do, I feel that it's all worth it."[9]

David Bogle (Ricky Nelson)

On November 17, 1985, Ricky Nelson made his final appearance at London's Royal Albert Hall. David Bogle had a chance to attend but didn't: "It's my biggest regret in life. My best friend went, but I stupidly said, 'Oh, I've got no money; I'll go next time.' There never would be another time. I still ache today. I become a bigger fan every day. I love the man so much."[10] Even though Ricky Nelson was a massive star in the late '50s and early '60s, his legacy is often forgotten. Bogle aims to change that with his portrayal of the teen idol. These days, Nelson is his main tribute, but for ten years, he paid homage to Buddy Holly and Elvis Presley. He admitted, "I played Elvis in three shows: *Rock 'n' Roll Paradise*, *Elvis vs. Jerry Lee Lewis—The Showdown* and *The Buddy Presley Show*." *Rock 'n' Roll Paradise* eventually offered him the chance to play a role full-time, and surprisingly they asked Bogle to choose. His choice was Nelson. Bogle is still active with that production, but he has also enjoyed critical acclaim with *Travelin' Man—The Ricky Nelson Rock 'n' Roll Show*. Doug Altman, Nelson's former drummer, and Gary Hirstius, Nelson's former manager, have complimented him on his portrayal. Bogle admitted, "That is the ultimate accolade, to receive praise from people who knew Ricky personally."

Bogle was born on August 29, 1965, in Cuckfield, West Sussex, England. At nine years old, he purchased *The Sun Collection* by Elvis Presley on cassette, which led him down the roots, Americana and rockabilly path. He declared, "My passion has always been '50s and '60s rock and roll. Elvis, Ricky Nelson, Buddy Holly, Gene Vincent and Eddie Cochran were my favorites and still are. Then in my teens, in the late '70s/early '80s, we had a massive rock and roll revival on the charts in the U.K. with The Stray Cats, Shakin' Stevens, The Jets, Matchbox, and The Darts all having hits. [Bogle then became a fan of those acts.] I always wanted to start a rock and roll band but, living in the country, I could never find friends who wanted to join me. I was a late starter in the music scene. When I entered a talent contest sponsored by the local newspaper, *The East Grinstead Observer*, I was 32. I performed an Elvis medley backed by the ConChord Big Band. I beat nine competitors at the Chequer Mead Theatre in East Grinstead, West Sussex, and won 100 English pounds. I was hooked then."

In March 1998, Bogle competed on the BBC TV show *Whatever You Want*, and won the opportunity to play Holly for one night in the West End stage show *Buddy: The Musical*: "It was one of the best times of my life. However, I didn't want to just give tribute to one artist and found I could perform as others, with equal authenticity. I loved attending rock and roll theater shows and always said to myself, 'I can do that.'" He stuck with the Holly act but also added Presley to his roster:

Four. Pop–Rock and Roll Icons

David Bogle began his career paying tribute to both Elvis Presley and Buddy Holly, but these days he concentrates on portraying his idol Ricky Nelson. Drummer Spencer Lingwood is also pictured (photograph by Neil R. Smith; courtesy David Bogle).

"As a lifelong Elvis fan, it seemed the obvious route to go down. I could do the voice, had the look and the image, and it was easy to get work as everyone wanted an Elvis tribute."

He recalled an embarrassing moment: "'G.I. Blues' had been requested at one of my shows, and I thought, 'That's a good one. I know that, easy.' I had it on a backing track, but then I realized that I didn't know it at all. The joy of the microphone is you can stifle your voice to make it sound like you are singing the words. I still got applause, though. I knew the tune, just not the words, and I still haven't learned them." Around the same time, Bogle played rock and roll in the pubs and clubs around South East England: "When I started out, my parents followed me everywhere. They were so supportive, as was my wife."

During his time as Presley, Bogle traveled to Tennessee to visit Memphis, Nashville and the Smoky Mountains: "One day in Nashville, it decided to pour so hard that we dove into the Hard Rock Café on Broadway, just to get out of the rain. We sat and ordered, and as I took the first bite of my huge burger, Scotty Moore walked past me on his way back from the men's room. He then went over and sat next to D.J. Fontana and Sam Phillips. I thought I had surely died and gone to Heaven. My wife said, 'You have to go and speak to them,' so I plucked up the courage. They were all complete gentlemen. Scotty gladly posed with me for a photo. They were in Nashville because they were being inducted into the Musicians' Hall of Fame. Thank the Lord it was raining hard that day."

After portraying the King of Rock and Roll for ten years, Bogle got disillusioned by the scene, especially the constant need to compete against one another at conventions. He wanted to pay homage to Nelson but wondered if he'd find an audience. The musical *Rock 'n' Roll Paradise* offered him the opportunity, and his first performance as Nelson was in front of 1000 people at the Tonbridge Music Weekend in Kent, England: "I realized I had nothing for stage clothing, so I visited charity shops to purchase Ricky-type gear, and the tribute was born. Having been a fan of his since childhood, thanks to my dad constantly playing 'Poor Little Fool' and 'Hello Mary Lou,' that really was a dream come true."

These days, venues around England, Scotland and Wales are all part of his tour itinerary: "I love old historic theaters, so whenever I play them, I walk around the whole venue looking at the box office, the auditorium, backstage, the private boxes and the [architectural] design. The most popular show I'm in today is *Rock 'n' Roll Paradise*, where I do 60 to 70 dates a year." His own musical, *Travelin' Man—The Ricky Nelson Rock 'n' Roll Show*, occupies the rest of his schedule. Its length is two 55-minute sets plus encores: "We set the first half of the show in the '50s where we do the rockabilly [material]. Then in the second set, we recreate one of his last shows, where we do all the big hits with more of an '80s sound: 'Travelin' Man,' 'Poor Little Fool,' 'It's Late,' 'Hello Mary Lou,' 'Stood Up' and 'Believe What You Say.' You have to include the big hits when doing a tribute show because, more often than not, you are performing to theatergoers rather than fans of the artist you are portraying. Luckily for me, no one else is doing Ricky Nelson." Bogle's all-time favorite track of Nelson's is "Just a Little Too Much." He mentioned, "*UK Rock 'n' Roll Magazine* said the version from my album *Beyond My Dreams* was as good as the original."

The best advice that Bogle ever received was from a fellow performer who told him to take any and all gigs: "I thought it odd at first but then realized it's like an apprenticeship. No two audiences or venues are the same, so you always have to give your best. I took every gig offered to me in the early days, and I played some utter dumps, but I don't regret any of them because I look at how far I've come. I'm now playing in some beautiful arenas. I spent those years perfecting my voice, my craft and my show. Now, preparation for me is easy. It comes with experience. I used to get so nervous where I would run to the loo at the last minute. I just gave myself a good talking-to: 'Calm down, it's not you they have come to see but the character you are playing. Just focus on being that person as best you can.' My own advice helped a lot. When I see an audience on its feet for my show that no one else is doing anywhere, it makes me proud of what I've set out to do."

Scott Hinds (Carl Perkins)

Many tribute artists have a background in theater and have graced the stage of the popular musical *Million Dollar Quartet*. Between October 2013 and August 2016, Scott Hinds understudied for the roles of Carl Perkins and Jay Perkins. He then decided to concentrate all his efforts on making his band, The Royal Hounds, a success. Since then, they have gained critical acclaim, including appearances on the Americana radio charts and playing rockabilly festivals worldwide, such as the Viva Las Vegas Rockabilly Weekender. In 2015, Hinds was hired by Viva Las Vegas promoter Tom Ingram. Hinds said, "I was emceeing a pinup pageant in Las Vegas [and] Tom was a judge. He liked my style in making the girls feel comfortable on stage and not objectified, so he invited me to host all the swimwear competitions and to introduce several bands at Viva. Through the years, my responsibilities have increased, and now I run the pool stage as well."[11]

Growing up, Hinds listened to and loved music from the '40s and '50s. In 1994 when the movie soundtrack *The Mask* was released, it made a deep impression upon him: "I'd never heard or at least been truly moved by Big Band swing before. It just spoke to me." Hinds wore the CD out because he played it so much. In high school, he delved into the blues and rockabilly. As a sophomore, he discovered rockabilly when he

You Sound Just Like…

Before Scott Hinds played Carl Perkins in the musical *Million Dollar Quartet*, he was an eighth-grade English teacher (photograph by Bill Foster; courtesy Scott Hinds).

Four. Pop–Rock and Roll Icons

saw Brian Setzer on VH1: "My jaw just dropped, and I remember thinking it might be the greatest thing I'd ever seen."[12] Setzer is a major musical influence, as is Hank Williams Sr.

Around the same time, Hinds also began singing: "A teacher knew I played guitar and asked me to put on a lunchtime concert in the school's courtyard. I had never sung before, and not knowing any better, unfortunately, chose several songs that were hard to sing. My classmates felt it was necessary to tell me how bad I was, and it gave me a fear of singing for a year. I tried to force myself to overcome my fear by doing impressions of other singers, such as old gravelly-voiced blues guys or Hank Williams Sr. I eventually found my voice and comfort in singing by trying to copy Michael Bublé. His voice is closest to my natural singing voice, and once I clicked with that, I moved forward and developed my own style. Even though I perform roots music and rockabilly, people often compare my singing style to Bruce Dickinson of Iron Maiden."

At age 22, Hinds started playing upright bass: "I had been playing guitar since I was a young teenager, but when I saw Joe Fick and his band, The Dempseys, I knew I wanted to play bass. Joe let me put my tape recorder on stage to record their entire concerts and then stayed after shows to teach me stuff. I'd spend about four months learning every note he played until he'd pass back through Knoxville and show me more. One day, he said, 'Well, Scott, I don't know that there's anything more I can show you.' In my opinion, Joe is at the top of the rockabilly slap game, best in the world."

For nine years, Hinds taught writing and grammar at the Fort Loudon Middle School in Loudon, Tennessee. He started instructing sixth-grade students, then moved up to eighth-graders. "I was pursuing a music career at the same time. People used to joke that teaching was my second job. I was doing whatever it took to have a music career outside of teaching, sometimes at crazy levels. I remember being on tour [with The Royal Hounds] while I was teaching. I would play in one city, leave the gig at 2 a.m., drive through the night to get back to Knoxville, sleep an hour or two in the school's band room, teach all day, and then get back in my car and drive to the next city. That certainly was not sustainable."

In 2013, Hinds became aware of an open casting call for the musical *Million Dollar Quartet*, so he flew to New York City and auditioned: "I was certain that I wouldn't get the part. I figured I'd be up against a lot of classically trained actors with long résumés, and who was I? I was just a middle school teacher by day, musician by night, with only a local

You Sound Just Like...

dinner theater on my acting résumé. I didn't hear anything for months, and I had put it out of my mind when I got a call one day, on my lunch break as a teacher. They wanted me to move to Vegas that week to be an understudy for both Carl Perkins and Jay Perkins." He walked into the principal's office and resigned. She was very supportive of his decision, and by the next day, Hinds was preparing for the stage. For a year, he worked a side job in Vegas, teaching graphic design at a private school.

Harrah's in Las Vegas hosted the musical, and for the next three years, Hinds was part of the show. "I've always been an energetic frontman because I love getting a crowd going, but when I played Carl Perkins, I had to rein it in. I stayed understudy because I was the only person capable of covering both the roles [of Carl and Jay]. In 2016, I chose to leave because I had a new album coming out and sensed the show would be closing soon.

"*Million Dollar Quartet* was a life-changing experience. I got to see and do things through that show that I never dreamed I would ever do. One of my favorite memories was meeting D.J. Fontana." Regarding one of his most embarrassing moments while portraying Carl Perkins, Hinds mentioned, "I broke a string, mid-song, and I was told if that happened to grab the backup guitar. Well, that guitar had never been used, so it wasn't in tune. It was a train wreck, but I made it through."

After leaving *Million Dollar Quartet*, Hinds' main focus became recording and touring with his band, The Royal Hounds, a band formed in 2011. Its current members are Hinds, guitarist Matheus Canteri and drummer Nathan Place. They have regularly played at Robert's Western World, Johnny Cash's Kitchen and Saloon, The Nashville Palace and the American Legion (all in Nashville). "In Nashville, you're working for tips, so the road can be a lot more lucrative. We're actually more of a touring band." The Royal Hounds once headlined the Christmas tree lighting ceremony in downtown Knoxville and had an unfortunate mishap: "There were 3000 people there, and I decided to attempt what I'd seen on YouTube earlier that day. [While standing on my bass,] I lost my balance, and my foot slipped off of it, kicking out the bridge. Strings went flying everywhere, and a giant thud rang out throughout the city. I quickly threw down the bass, grabbed a guitar and kept singing. At the end of the song, the rest of the band launched into a new one while I went backstage and pieced the bass together.. Within minutes, I was back at it. I learned a valuable lesson that day. Don't try a new trick until you've practiced it at home."

An ideal set is around an hour and 15 minutes to an hour and a half, but they can play up to five hours of material. Unfortunately, Hinds often gets requests for songs that he doesn't know: "Sometimes I try my best if I think I can pull it off, and other times I'm honest and say, 'Ma'am, I just don't think I would do it justice. Is there something else we can play?' Although, my favorite way to handle a bad request is by saying, 'Well, sir, we don't know that Justin Bieber song, but here's one from his second album.' Then we'll play whatever we were going to play next, such as 'Ghost Riders in the Sky.' People who know better laugh, and people who don't, think: 'Wow, I didn't know Justin Bieber did that song.'"

Naturally, the trio covers a lot of rockabilly tunes, but they predominately feature originals, written mainly by Hinds: "I really started focusing on my songwriting skills shortly after I started playing upright bass. I wanted the band to be taken seriously. 'I'm in Love with a Zombie' is the first song that represented my voice as a writer. It's pretty 'out of the box,' having been inspired by Cuban music. The song really set me down a path of not writing rockabilly or listening to it for inspiration. If I write songs that don't sound like the genre, then all of a sudden, we become the most unique-sounding rockabilly band around."

Hinds admitted, "I'd describe The Royal Hounds' sound as quirky rock and roll. While we started out as a rockabilly band, we've moved quite a bit beyond that. We play everything from Latin-style songs to Russian circus music. We aim to do mostly originals, but whatever covers we do, we put our own twist on them and make them our own. Fans almost expect that."

Ty Stone (James Brown)

The Sunset Ballroom in Chicago played host to many legendary artists, including B.B. King, Gladys Knight and the Pips, Martha Reeves and the Vandellas, The Temptations and Bobby Blue Bland. Ty Stone's uncle owned the venue, so Stone had the opportunity to see several of those acts. Music was at the forefront of his childhood. In school, his band frequently paid tribute to James Brown. Experiencing Brown's high-octane live performances convinced Stone that he had to be a professional entertainer. Since 2007, Stone has been thrilling audiences with his show *The James Brown Experience*. Brown's widow, Tomi Rae Hynie, endorses the homage. In 2016, at his concert at the Green Valley Ranch Resort Spa and Casino in Las Vegas, Hynie accompanied him on background vocals.

You Sound Just Like...

James Cagney was Stone's first tribute because he loved the way he danced like a puppet. Then at age eight, after seeing the movie *Viva Las Vegas*, he began paying tribute to Elvis Presley. In fact, the first song he ever sang was "Hound Dog." Even though his father eventually bought him a guitar, he didn't think Stone had any talent.

Stone impersonated James Brown on his front porch for the neighbors. As a high school freshman, he auditioned for the school talent contest by singing tracks from the album *Live at the Apollo*: "The students broke the door down. They went ballistic. I couldn't get off the stage."[13] After that, his band participated in every local talent contest. To incorporate Brown's latest dance moves into their act, they combined their money and then chose one band member to attend his local concert. On six different occasions, Stone got to see Brown live on stage. His first experience was when his parents snuck him backstage at his uncle's nightclub. He never forgot that night and became a lifelong student of the Godfather of Soul. Brown, Wilson Pickett, Jackie Wilson and Joe Tex are Stone's musical influences.

Prior to his portrayal of James Brown, Ty Stone played guitar behind such legendary acts as Gene Chandler and Jackie Wilson. Wilson would often give him vocal lessons onstage (courtesy Ty Stone).

At the Sunset Ballroom, the ten-year-old Stone saw many big names in concert. Those shows made quite an impression on him. When he got a little older, he played guitar at the Auditorium Theater in Chicago and toured the South (known as the Chitlin' Circuit) with Wilson, Johnnie Taylor, The Staple Singers and Gene Chandler. Stone was very respectful toward these legendary acts. Knight was concerned about

Four. Pop–Rock and Roll Icons

Stone, asking about his grades in school and if he was saving any money. Wilson gave vocal lessons on stage. Stone recalled, "He called me Baby Brother and always said to me, 'Do that James Brown thang.' I would sing 'I Feel Good,' and he would laugh."

For 15 years, Stone was addicted to drugs. He acknowledged: "I lived on the streets of Chicago, eating at shelters and out of Burger King's dumpsters. One day, I said, 'Drugs aren't going to allow you to have anything. There is no bottom. You will never hit bottom. It is a black hole.' I asked God to take the taste for drugs out of my mouth. He did, and I walked away. I never looked back, and I thank God every day." Law enforcement also helped him get sober by telling him what life in prison would be like if he didn't turn his life around.

In early 2007, a promoter and friend told Stone he should create a tribute show devoted to Brown. *The James Brown Experience* was then launched. Stone's ten-piece band plus background singers paid homage to soul revues, similar to those once held at the Apollo Theater in Harlem or the Regal Theater in Chicago. The first half of his show is dedicated to the music of Ray Charles, The Blues Brothers, Stevie Wonder, Etta James and Wilson Pickett, and the second half focuses entirely on Brown. Stone admitted, "I only play theaters, casinos, corporate and private events, and festivals because my guys are the best that money can buy, and I must pay them as such. I choose to work only about twice a month as it is a hassle moving the show around."

Most of his costumes are tailor-made, and it takes about two hours for him to do his hair and makeup: "I have a guy, who did the wigs for the movie *Hairspray*, take care of mine, and as far as makeup I learned how to do it myself thanks to some drag queens who instructed me." It then takes him an extra half-hour to get into James Brown mode—to build up the appropriate amount of attitude and swagger. "I picked James because of that soulful thing he had, that emotion. He kind of hypnotized his audience."[14]

During the 90-minute spectacular, Stone has five costume changes and never stops moving with leaps, splits and spins: "The energy comes from within, and the band keeps me moving, especially my drummer and bass player. The moves are the hardest because I don't count steps. I just dance. The voice is easier because that's all attitude." Songs such as "I Feel Good," "Papa's Got a Brand New Bag" and "Living in America" are always included in the setlists, but a few of his personal favorites to sing are "Cold Sweat" and "I Got the Feelin'." He admitted, "Those were the songs I learned off the radio." He videotapes his performances, and after each show, he reviews the tape. Stone tries hard to keep Brown's legacy alive, and in the process he has perfected his act: "I do James Brown better than I do myself."[15]

Pete Hutton (Ral Donner)

Pete Hutton primarily pays tribute to three different artists: Elvis Presley, Ricky Nelson and Ral Donner. On November 17, 1985, several weeks before Nelson was killed in an airplane accident, he played one of his last concerts at the Royal Albert Hall in London, and Hutton was in attendance. It was an experience he never forgot.

These days, gigs are plentiful for Hutton and his band, the Beyonders, named after a Spider-Man character. So far, they have recorded eight albums. Hutton acknowledged, "I started writing my own songs around 2001. Showcasing your own material identifies your musical

Pete Hutton used James Intveld's band as backing at the Rockin' E Jamboree in Green Bay, Wisconsin. Hutton's songs were challenging for the band to learn with only one rehearsal, so they suggested that he sing some of Intveld's songs (courtesy Daniel Gerrits).

heroes. Nearly every song I've recorded, you can hear my influences, which include Elvis and James Intveld."[16] Hutton describes many of his originals as potential movie songs: "Elvis could have easily performed any of these in his films. 'Lure of a Star' sounds like it could have been in *G.I. Blues* while 'She's Mean and She's Evil' could have been out of *King Creole*." He has also covered a few Presley tunes on his studio releases: "His Latest Flame," "Pocket Full of Rainbows," "A Fool Such as I," "Ain't That Lovin' You Baby" and "What's She Really Like."

At six years old, Hutton began singing. The first tune he ever sang was "Simple Simon Says" in front of a wedding party. Ten years later, he took up the guitar: "I had a few lessons, but I wasn't really learning what I wanted to play. I was shown some chords but basically taught myself. The first songs I sang while playing guitar were 'That's All Right' and 'Blue Suede Shoes.'" His other musical influences include Billy Fury, Donner, Nelson, Eddie Cochran, Cliff Richard, The Recalls, Ray Melton, Eddie Cash and Gary Hodge.

His first tribute was to Presley: "I've always had people tell me I sound as close to Elvis as Ral Donner. When I sing Elvis' songs, I hear his voice going through my head and feel a presence inside me. I don't really get into character before I perform."

He added, "I've always loved the Elvis image, and I really do sound like him. Many people have been fooled. My parents were once at a red [stop] light, and a woman pulled alongside them while [my version of] 'His Latest Flame' played. The woman said, 'You can't beat a bit of Elvis.' My mom said, 'Yes, but that's my son.' The woman replied, 'Never.'"

Hutton also pays homage to Nelson and Donner: "Ricky had a great soft tone to his voice. Elvis moved around with all his hip thrusts, but Rick didn't really have to do a lot. His voice said everything. 'Travelin' Man' and 'Fools Rush In' are my favorite tracks." On October 6, 2012, Hutton paid tribute to Nelson at the Hemsby Rock'n'Roll Weekender in Great Yarmouth, United Kingdom; afterward, the promoter approached him about doing another show. Hutton suggested a set that combined his originals with tunes by Presley sound-alikes, but the promoter wasn't interested: "He said because the Ricky Nelson tribute had been such a success, it would be good to play another, so I suggested Ral Donner, but with a small twist: I would add in a few Vince Everett songs. Playing Ral's songs was a dream come true for me because no one had ever paid tribute to him before. 'I Got Burned' and 'Silver and Gold' are my favorites of his." Typically, Hutton chooses the songs he will perform: "I aim for a few that are easily recognizable, a few that are rare gems, and then some real rockin' songs, along with a few ballads. That way, you end up with a nice balance."

Festivals and clubs are his main venues, and the show's length ranges from 45 to 90 minutes. Hutton's tributes are very successful, but he's also revered for the work he does with his group, the Beyonders, which was formed in early 2001: "Our name came from my sons Aaron and Joshua. They were watching a Spider-Man cartoon, and one character was named the Beyonder. We really started as just a recording band, but after the release of our first album, *Once Bitten Twice Shy*, I started getting phone calls from clubs asking if we could play live." In his sets, he alternates between originals and covers. "Once I was asked to perform 'Stray Cat Strut.' I kept saying I'd throw it in at the end of the night, hoping that I could finish without performing it because I never knew the lyrics. However, the guy kept asking for it, so I ended up singing it with my own lyrics—off the top of my head. After the show, the guy remarked, 'Wow, what version was that?' I said, 'Those were the original lyrics, but they were changed at the recording session.' I'll never know how I got away with that."

In August 2010, Hutton had another memorable experience when he played the Rockin' E Jamboree in Green Bay, Wisconsin: "On arrival, I had been loaned a guitar. James Intveld's band was going to back me, and they had been learning my songs. In rehearsal, the band asked if I could perform some of James' songs since mine were proving a little difficult to nail down. James walked in and said, 'Is that [the guitar] that they have given you to play? You can't use that on stage. Here, use mine.' His guitar player, Storm, then told him, 'Pete's going to perform some of your songs as well.' James said, 'Fine,' as he was singing some Ricky Nelson tunes. After my show, James walked up to me and said, 'You sound more like me than I do.' Thanks to him, I made a few more fans that evening."

Five

Women Who Rock

Tammi Savoy (Diana Ross)

Lance Lipinsky wanted to add female backing vocalists to his band, similar to Ray Charles' Raelettes, and he would christen them The Lovettes. Darcy Jo Wood and Jessica Lyons were already singing background for him, but then, in 2014, he contacted Vavoom Pinups to see if the owner knew of a lady who looked like Diana Ross for his music video "So Real." Tammi Savoy was suggested and then recruited. Initially, he would have her lip-sync, but once he heard her sing and witnessed her chemistry with the other two gals, he decided to hire her. From then on, she was a featured vocalist. In Lipinsky's shows, a section was added where the three female vocalists took turns singing the lead. One of Savoy's main tunes was LaVern Baker's "Jim Dandy." For a few years, Savoy had success with Lipinsky's band. At various theaters and rockabilly festivals around the country, she made a name for herself. Eventually, though, the spotlight shone on her solo talent, and she went from the background to the foreground. This happened thanks to Chris Casello. They had met in Lipinsky's band, as Casello was sometimes hired to play lead guitar. In late 2017, an impromptu version of "Jim Dandy," at one of Casello's Chicago gigs, led to a recording collaboration between the two in his basement studio. Those efforts turned into an EP; gigs followed, and in October 2020, they released their first full-length CD, *That Rock 'n' Roll Rhythm!*

Tammi Savoy was born on August 5, 1985, in St. Paul, Minnesota. It is her stage name, which is a combined homage to singer Tammi Terrell and Savoy Records. At the age of three, Savoy began singing in the church choir. Throughout her childhood, thanks to her father's radio station preferences on family road trips, she was introduced to various genres of music, including soul, Motown and rhythm and blues. Incidentally, singing runs in the family since Savoy's two older brothers are part of the R&B group Next. These days, Savoy's husband is often seen at her shows photographing the glamorous singer, and their daughter sometimes sings a duet with her on stage. In 2019, they sang The Collins Kids' classic "Hop, Skip, and Jump" at the Bourbon and Brass Speakeasy in Evanston, Illinois. A video can be seen on Savoy's YouTube channel.

One of Savoy's main inspirations is Diana Ross, and she's paid tribute to Ross on three occasions: "I made sure that I had the most sparkly gown and the '60s hairstyle and makeup. I grew up listening to The Supremes, and I have always loved them. I loved their style and grace, and I used to imagine that I was on stage performing with them.[1]

"I have not seen Diana Ross in concert yet, but I would love to. I also would like to meet her and ask her to share a few makeup tips with me. I would especially like to know how she applied those lashes back then."

"Ain't No Mountain High Enough" is one of Savoy's favorites to sing: "I love holding out the long notes, and I like to dance around my house while singing it. As far as my favorite that I have sung on stage, I would have to say 'Someday We'll Be Together,' because I love singing the trills and ad libs." Savoy also loves Ella

On November 17, 2019, Tammi Savoy paid special tribute to Ruth Brown in a set at the UK's Rhythm Riot. Other than Savoy, four female vocalists were featured—Shanda Cisneros, Miss Lily Moe, Sister Suzie, and L'il Miss Mary. Savoy sang two tunes—"I Wanna Do More" and "Wild Wild Young Men," then took the lead on the All-Star assemblage of "As Long as I'm Moving" (courtesy Tammi Savoy).

Five. Women Who Rock

Fitzgerald and Sarah Vaughan: "Their voices sound like an instrument to me. They do things with their voices that I have never been able to achieve. I love their scatting styles as well."

In 2014, Savoy began singing professionally. It started when the photographer and owner of Vavoom Pinups, Heather Stumpf Popio, was contacted by Lance Lipinsky. He wanted to add a third voice to his troupe of backing vocalists. Savoy recalled, "I met Lance because I had done a photoshoot with Heather [which turned into] a pinup calendar for my hubby. Lance wanted someone who looked like Diana Ross for his upcoming music video, for his song, 'So Real.' Heather sent him my info, and we had a brief conversation before he sent me the song. He asked questions like, 'Can you sing?' I replied, 'I can hold a note.' Then he said, 'Can you dance?' I answered, 'I've got a little rhythm.' Lance hired me to appear in his video and lip-sync with The Lovettes. When we started shooting the video, Darcy, Jessica and I started singing together, and it was instant harmony. We never did lip-sync. After the first take, Jessica looked at me and said, 'So … what are you doing Saturday?' That was Memorial Day 2014."

Eventually, Lipinsky showcased the ladies' talents in their own segment in his shows and helped create a solo show for them to shine; the latter is called *Leaders of the Pack*. Darcy Jo Wood also helped to get the show up and running. Savoy remembered, "I suffered from bad stage fright, but gradually I started to feel more comfortable up there, so we began to expand our routines."[2]

She added, "In the beginning, there was a choreographer for a few songs, but later on, as tunes were added, we started working on dance moves together. Darcy usually chose the songs, and we worked out harmonies on our own, by ear. I usually sang the alto parts, but we switched it up every once in a while. As far as outfits, we switched from '40s to '50s to '60s costumes during the show."

Savoy has modeled for Stop Staring and Prettie Lanes clothing lines. One of the biggest highlights of The Lovettes' career was their inclusion in the PBS special *Doo Wop Generation*. During the program, they sang "He's So Fine," "Dedicated to the One I Love" and "One Fine Day."

Savoy has also provided background vocals for Elvis Tribute Artists: "I was a sub for Darcy when she was part of the EAS Band, so the first [one I sang with] was Brandon Bennett. I have had the opportunity to perform with several ETAs. Now I sing backup for Dean Z. I love singing with them because I enjoy having the chance to sing harmonies. It's always fun to listen to the backup parts in Elvis' songs and then figure out the harmonies. Some of them are quite challenging, but I love a good challenge." A few of the other ETAs she has worked with include Cody Slaughter, Victor Trevino Jr., and Bill Cherry.

In January 2018, Savoy decided to become a full-time singer and develop a solo act. The transition happened rather quickly and spontaneously, primarily due to the overwhelmingly warm response she received from the audience at a Chris Casello show: "My hubby and I went out for his birthday; Chris was performing at the Honky Tonk BBQ in Chicago. Chris asked me to sing a song during his set with the Corsairs, and we chose 'Jim Dandy' because it was one of the songs we performed together with Lance. I had met Chris when he subbed on guitar for Lance. Afterward, the crowd kept shouting for more, but we didn't know any more songs. I mentioned to Chris that I wanted to come out with a 45 RPM record, and he said he could help me with that, so we started rehearsing songs in his basement."

Casello remembered, "They bought my CD and called me the next day and asked if I would do a record on her, and I said, 'Let's do more than a record. Let's do a group!'"[3] Savoy added, "Chris recorded the rehearsals, and the feedback was so great that it turned into gig offers. Ultimately those are the recordings that you hear on our EP *Rhythm & Roll*. [Incidentally,] that was our first rehearsal." The 2018 Nashville Boogie was her first significant festival with Casello.

The band consists of Savoy, Casello, upright bassist Jesse Woelfel and drummer Russ DeLuca. Their setlists pay tribute to both the famous and lesser-known ladies of rhythm and blues. Savoy thinks it's essential to showcase women of the bygone era who didn't get the credit they deserved, such as Varetta Dillard, Annisteen Allen and Priscilla Bowman. "I would say the song selection is a group effort. We also get recommendations from a lot of people. We usually do a rehearsal to see what sounds good, and then it goes on the setlist if we like it." Savoy has even written a few tunes, including "I Want Your Good Lovin': "I wrote it one day after watching a documentary about Amy Winehouse on Netflix. I think it really motivated me because I wrote that song in about 30 minutes. I usually start on a song and come back to finish the rest, but this was the first time I wrote an entire song all at once. It doesn't come super-easy for me. I have to be in the mood."

The American crowds have applauded Savoy's efforts, but she's also gained a following in Australia and England. In 2019, Savoy received the highest rockabilly honor, an Ameripolitan Award for Rockabilly Female of the Year. She was pleasantly surprised that she had such a large fan base that voted for her: "I love what the Ameripolitan Music Awards stand for. It's all about keeping roots music alive, and I feel like that is what I'm doing every time I step on stage."[4]

Julie Myers (Stevie Nicks)

Stevie Nicks has not seen Julie Myers' spot-on tribute, but Nicks' best friend Mary Torre has. According to Myers, "Early in my career, she came to a show in Florida. Mary was impressed with me, but not with the band. Unfortunately, we had not rehearsed, and I had never performed with them before."[5] Since then, theaters, cruise ships, casinos and performing arts centers have lined up to book Myers. There are two different productions to choose from: *Nearly Nicks* and *Dreams: A Classic Rock Fantasy.* In the latter, she shares the stage with Johnny Moroko as Mick Jagger and Martin D. Andrew as Rod Stewart. She also sings a few of her originals. All the years of hard work have paid off as critics have hailed Myers' tribute as one of the best and most authentic representations ever given to Nicks and her career.

Myers started singing at the age of five: "I sang 'I'm Leaving on a Jet Plane' by Peter, Paul and Mary in the school talent show. My brother accompanied me on guitar, and I won first place." She took

Julie Myers covers all aspects of Stevie Nicks' career, from the early days with Lindsey Buckingham to Fleetwood Mac to her solo career, as well as her duets. Myers's favorite song to sing is "Landslide." In fact, it was her wedding song (courtesy Julie Myers).

singing lessons but also studied several forms of dance: ballet, tap, and jazz. Her mother was especially supportive of her musical aspirations: "She was a total stage mom and worked for many years as a crossing guard to pay for my dancing and singing lessons. It was something my mom always wanted to do as a child but could not afford it, so she lives vicariously through me." Elvis Presley went to school with her mother: "She was a junior when he was a senior at Humes High in Memphis and sang with the orchestra at the junior-senior prom. She was asked to sit in with the band for only one song, but when she finished, Elvis came up, put his arm around her shoulder, gave it a little squeeze and said, 'Good job, Peggy.' My mom remembered him bringing his guitar to school and playing it outside on breaks. I don't think anyone at the time had any idea he would be so big. He was kind of thought of as a greaser. He wore his hair longer than most of the other guys and was a loner."

Myers attended college for a bit, majoring in drama before she dropped out to pursue her dreams of becoming a singer. Her professional career began in the early '80s, performing at Memphis theme parks. She moved to Hollywood, then showcased her talent in Las Vegas, where she danced and was a featured backup vocalist in productions such as *Melinda: The First Lady of Magic*, *Playboy's Girls of Rock and Roll* and *Legends in Concert*. She also toured the country with the latter two shows.

A fall from scaffolding almost ended her career. For the next ten years, she assisted with the caretaking duties of her father, who had been stricken with Alzheimer's. After his death in 2007, she looked for a way to get back into performing: "I had gone back to school to study Aesthetics, but when I dyed my hair and cut my bangs, people started telling me everywhere I went that I resembled Stevie Nicks, so I took that as a sign from God."

Since the late 1970s, Myers has been a fan of Fleetwood Mac. *Rumours* is one of her all-time favorite albums, and Nicks, Linda Ronstadt, Tanya Tucker, Don Henley, Bonnie Raitt and Sheryl Crow are some of her musical influences. Her first gig as Nicks was in a show called *Kopy Catz* hosted by the Morongo Casino in Cabazon, California. Individuals portraying Barbra Streisand, Frank Sinatra, Michael Jackson and Ozzy Osbourne were also featured. To prepare for the role, Myers watched a lot of videos and listened to Nicks' CDs non-stop: "I listened for the way she used certain tones in her voice and how she pronounced certain words."

Myers created a tribute show, *Nearly Nicks*, which features a six-piece band and a backup singer. Her husband assists with stage production. Nicks' entire career is covered, from her Fleetwood Mac days to her solo career to her duets with Tom Petty, Don Henley and others. Myers said, "I typically choose the biggest hits and the ones most familiar to the audience, such as 'Landslide,' 'Rhiannon,' 'Dreams,' 'Edge of Seventeen,' 'Stand Back' and 'Gold Dust Woman.' I have sung these songs so much that I rarely mess up on lyrics, but it happens. If I swap the verses or forget a double chorus, I can usually fudge my way through. We don't take requests in our shows because it is tightly produced with click tracks to help the musicians stay on track with what is happening on the video screens."

Her other creative endeavor is *Dreams: A Classic Rock Fantasy*. Myers co-wrote it with Martin D. Andrew, who stars as Rod Stewart. Mick Jagger is portrayed by Johnny Moroko. In the show, a man falls asleep and the audience goes with him in his dreams. He meets Nicks, Stewart and Jagger, and they sing his favorite songs. At the end of the musical, Myers showcases five of her original tunes. Audience members then have the opportunity to purchase her CD, *Rock On/Fearless Journey*, on which those originals appear. It was recorded in Nashville. Reba McEntire's drummer, Tommy Harden, was her bandleader, and Michael Rojas, a keyboardist who has worked with Nicks, was also on it.

In 2017, *Dreams: A Classic Rock Fantasy* won Best Show of the Year in Branson, Missouri. Myers admitted, "I've come to appreciate Stevie Nicks as probably one of the greatest songwriters and live entertainers of our time, and I'm honored when people tell me I've done a good job of replicating that."[6]

Laura West (Ann-Margret)

Jake Slater often shares the stage with his fiancée Laura West. They both love Elvis Presley and all things retro. Her tributes to Marilyn Monroe, Ann-Margret and Priscilla Presley fit in nicely with his homage to Elvis. West stated, "We have fun doing our own shows but really love our duets together [including 'You're the Boss,' which was originally sung by Elvis and Ann]. The audiences [often tell us] they can see and feel our chemistry."[7] She added, "Elvis and his music brought us together." In 2018, they got engaged at Graceland. On the rare occasion when West hasn't been on the same bill as Slater, her duet partner is either Victor Trevino Jr. or Cote Deonath. Performing takes up the

You Sound Just Like...

majority of her time, but West also models for magazines and websites and has her own vintage boutique, Eclectic West.

West started singing at a very young age. She became an instant Elvis Presley fan at age two, thanks to a cassette of his music that her father gave her. Her top Elvis songs are "Baby, Let's Play House," "Fame and Fortune" and "My Happiness." She also has fond memories of listening to rock and roll and oldies. While enrolled in school, she was a competitive gymnast and cheerleader. A bit later, she participated in beauty pageants, where her platform was ending animal cruelty.

Her first gig as Marilyn Monroe was at a banquet event: "I searched through many photos and videos, watched all the movies and many documentaries about her. I feel it's important to learn as much as you can about the icon. My favorite [Monroe] movies are *Bus Stop* and *Don't Bother to Knock*, and my favorite song of hers is 'I Wanna Be Loved by You.' I have always admired her." Monroe- and Priscilla Presley–inspired photoshoots occurred before West portrayed them on stage or at a meet-and-greet. She commented, "Marilyn was the first photoshoot. I was then encouraged by many to pursue tribute work as well."

Attention to detail has proven vital to West's tributes. She has

Laura West prepared for the role of Ann-Margret by watching and studying her movies. Photographs were also instrumental in helping recreate the actress' iconic looks. West's favorite song to sing is "You're the Boss," which is usually performed as a duet with her fiancé Jake Slater (right), who portrays Elvis Presley (courtesy Laura West).

brought many of the iconic styles of Monroe, Priscilla Presley and Ann-Margret back to life: "I have custom-made outfits [crafted] by a seamstress as well as items I've put together. I make my own unique hair bows, hair flowers and other accessories. My favorite looks that I've recreated of Priscilla's were with my fiancé when we were on our way to Palm Springs and also at the Honeymoon House in Palm Springs." West's onstage personas are helping her utilize her bachelor's degree in Fashion Merchandising and Design from Meredith College in Raleigh, North Carolina.

In her spare time, she has a passion for collecting antiques, which has provided her with the opportunity to open her own store. West finds beauty in making what's old new again, mainly through her tributes: "I adore bringing memories back to people and creating new ones."

Lisa Irion (Cher)

Recognition as one of the world's top Cher tribute artists isn't Lisa Irion's only claim to fame. With over 30 years in the entertainment industry, she also has experience in theater, voice-over work and TV commercials. She first paid homage to Cher in 2003. In 2006 and 2007, Irion was awarded international tribute industry awards for her Cher portrayal. Irion stated, "Although I'm obviously not her, I feel very blessed to touch some people that want to believe it's her—for a while."[8]

Irion was born in 1960 in Abbeville, Louisiana. Irion stated, "I can't remember a time when I didn't sing. As a toddler, I sang 'Moon Ridder' ['Moon River']."[9] At four years old, she started playing piano by ear: "I could play with one hand the melody of anything that I could hum, with very few mistakes." The first song she played was "I'm in the Mood for Love." However, she took lessons two years later, then on and off throughout college. Her musical influences are Dr. John, Sade, The Neville Brothers, Steely Dan, Bonnie Raitt, Grover Washington Jr. and Jon Cleary.

Irion's main clientele is casinos and private and corporate events: "I also sometimes play theaters at high-end retirement communities." Typically, the show is 90 minutes in length. She admitted, "As Cher, most of the time I play alone although I have worked alongside tributes to Frank Sinatra, Elvis Presley, Elton John, John Lennon and Rod Stewart. I did a show called *The Divas of Rock and Roll* with Connie Garrett as Tina Turner. As Patsy, I try to perform with Johnny Cash Tribute Artist Bennie Wheels in *The Cash and Cline Show*. I find the duo shows more fun for both the artists and the audience."

You Sound Just Like...

In January 2003, she showcased her tribute to Cher for the very first time: "It was a *Legends*-style show called *Superstars in Concert*, which Parris Plaisance, an Elvis Tribute Artist, and I co-produced at a community theater. [Cher, Elvis Presley, and Frank Sinatra were the featured acts.] The audience response was really good. We sold out, and it resulted in getting local corporate work. I got mixed reviews from the area newspaper critics. One raved about it while another was quite critical. I took the latter as constructive criticism and worked on those areas." For a year and a half, she did the show with Plaisance. Irion acknowledged, "I still don't think I've perfected any of my Cher tribute. It's such an ongoing process. I'd say the hardest aspect is her movement. I'm a different body type than her, and I don't move nearly as gracefully as she does, so it's difficult to walk like her, dance like her, etc."

Intensive training and extensive studying of Cher were necessary for Irion to prepare for the role: "I watched interviews and her TV show, which helped me get a grasp of her on- and off-stage personas, speech patterns and facial expressions. Watching her concerts and music videos helped me learn her moves, gestures and stage personality." It's a lengthy process to complete her Cher transformation: "I spend up to two hours in makeup. The wigs are very easy to style, so that takes very little time. I have blue eyes and blond hair, so brown contact lenses and wigs are a must. It took about three years to perfect my makeup. I eventually hired Marlene Stoller, an Emmy-nominated Hollywood makeup artist who specialized in character recreation. We conferenced online and by phone, and she helped me tweak the look a lot further. We loved talking about makeup and became pretty good friends. Sadly, she passed away in 2010. For a show, I also have to lay out all my costumes, wigs and jewelry, in a certain way, in the dressing room for quick changes. The max I have ever done is seven costume changes over a two-hour show. That was brutal, and I won't do that again. Most of the time, I use three or four costumes. I took a poll and discovered that audiences prefer fewer costume changes and more songs, so I'm developing a show that only uses two costumes."

All of her costumes are custom-made. Her first that resembled Cher's was the mirrored crop top and silver metallic pants from the *Believe* tour. Irion's favorite is the black cutout bodysuit with over-the-knee boots and a long curly wig, similar to what Cher wore in her music video "If I Could Turn Back Time": "It is the most requested and most slenderizing. Underneath, I wear opaque nude-colored spandex from my bra line to my ankles, and Cher's famous derriere tattoo is drawn on the spandex. Even up close, you can't tell that the spandex isn't skin. Without the spandex, there's no way I could or would wear that costume. Cher is a brave woman. It gets the biggest response from audiences."

As for the setlists, Irion concentrates on Cher's hits such as "The Shoop Shoop Song (It's in His Kiss)," "I Got You Babe," "If I Could Turn Back Time," "Believe" and a medley of "Half Breed," "Gypsies, Tramps, and Thieves," and "Dark Lady." Her favorites to sing are "Welcome to Burlesque," "because the arrangement is so campy and different from her typical songs," and "Just Like Jesse James," "because it is an audience favorite. I usually sit down on a barstool for that one. It is a welcome break, off my feet. I have had clients request

In a publicity photo for her tribute to Cher, Lisa Irion wears the infamous "If I Could Turn Back Time" costume. Its cutouts require Irion to wear nude-colored spandex underneath so she doesn't reveal too much (courtesy Lisa Irion).

songs that I didn't know, but as long as I could find a backing track or get the band to learn it, then I would [sing the song.]"

Cher has never seen Irion's tribute live: "The producer of the 2007 Cher Expo in Hilton Head, South Carolina, told me Cher requested a video of my performance. They confirmed that Cher's assistant accepted it when it was sent to her." Irion has seen Cher in concert: "I attended a show on the *Farewell* Tour when it came to my hometown of Lafayette, Louisiana. I won tickets in a Cher lookalike contest. The local news came to my house the day of the concert and filmed me getting into makeup as Cher. Before the concert, I had been hired to sing 'Happy Birthday,' as Cher, to the manager of the hockey team's husband in a VIP

You Sound Just Like...

suite at the Cajun Dome. The TV news crew followed me around at the concert as I walked the floor. Her video crew even put me on the Jumbotron. That was a fun night, and Cher was amazing."

Irion paid tribute to Patsy Cline with the full-length show *Crazy for Cline* in 2010. In 2005, she played her for the first time in a show called *Viva Las Divas*. Dolly Parton, Gloria Estefan and Cher were also featured. Irion portrayed all the characters. She revealed, "When I saw the video, I knew my Patsy needed more work. I was still tweaking my Cher act, so I tabled doing Patsy further until 2010. In 2015, I decided to dive in and put on a 90-minute show. My husband had commented that my natural voice was similar to hers, so I went with that. I researched the backstories to many of the songs, studied her speech patterns and the pitch and tone of her speaking voice, etc. I also studied every nuance of her voice and worked on it over and over again. The show sold out." The following year, the musical *Always Patsy Cline* showcased Irion's talent as the country legend for three weeks to sold-out audiences in Louisiana: "The reaction was very encouraging. I adore Patsy's songs and voice. My favorites of hers to sing are 'Gotta Lot of Rhythm in My Soul' because it is just so catchy and foot-stomping, plus the lyrics are fun, and 'You Belong to Me' because it's such a beautifully written ballad where the imagery of the lyrics take you to such lovely places."

In 2018, Irion joined forces with Johnny Cash Tribute Artist Bennie Wheels to create *The Cash and Cline Show*. In February of that same year, for two weekends at the Abbey Players Theater in Abbeville, Louisiana, Irion starred as Morticia Addams: "They were putting on *The Addams Family Musical*, and the director recruited me to audition for the role. My work schedule was light at the time, so I tried out and got the part. The character development didn't take very long. I was very familiar with Carolyn Jones as Morticia from the TV show, so I blended her characterization with my own. Due to choreography, I couldn't really move like her, that little shuffle, for most of my scenes, but I tried my best to convey that. I also tried to copy her look, so for makeup, it took about 45 minutes. Carolyn and I both have high foreheads and high cheekbones, so I played those up."

An embarrassing moment occurred during its run: "There was a scene where I'm seated on a bench, and Gomez is standing close behind me. His coat button got caught in the back of my wig, and when he moved, it yanked the wig halfway off my head. I immediately grabbed the top of my head where the wig was still on, looked down, and quickly pulled it back into place. It was now unsecured and still caught in his button. The audience was dying, laughing. Gomez is trying to free his button from my hair while we are still delivering our lines. His line was something to the effect, 'Tell me, what will it take for you to love me again?' I ad-libbed, 'I just want my hair back!' The audience was roaring by then. As he forcefully ripped the button off his jacket and from my wig, the button dangling with broken hair attached to it, he said, 'We're really splitting hairs now.' The audience lost it; they were laughing so hard. I don't know how we kept our composure, but we continued the scene as if nothing had happened. Luke Nettles, who played Gomez, was such a pro that he had the presence of mind to cradle the back of my head while I was being dipped backward during our tango number to make sure my wig didn't fall off. He made it look like part of the choreography. The hardest part for me was dancing to 'Tango De Amor.' I am not the most graceful person on the dance floor."

Irion had one of her most memorable experiences while she portrayed Cher: "I was booked to perform for a classic car show in Salina, Kansas. Salina coincidentally was having a Doo Wop Extravaganza show starring Kathy Young, Jimmy Clanton, Jay Traynor, The Contours and Jay Black from Jay and the Americans at the Bicentennial Center Arena the same weekend. Since I would be in town, the city booked me to open as Cher for the show. After my performance, I was invited to the green room backstage for a dinner buffet. While I was eating, Jimmy Clanton walked in and complimented me on my performance, chatting with me for a while. He was so nice. I just adore Jimmy. The Contours then arrived, and they addressed me like I was the real Cher, which was hilarious. When the show began, I took my seat, still dressed as Cher. With the finale of 'Goodnite, Sweetheart, Goodnite,' all the performers took the stage, and they also called me up from the audience. Jimmy and The Contours made room for me between them, and one of The Contours shared his microphone with me. Their smiles and friendliness immediately put me at ease. It was surreal because I grew up listening to their records, but I savored every minute."

Amberley Beatty (Patsy Cline)

ABBA, Shania Twain, Madonna, Patsy Cline, Connie Francis, Gretchen Wilson and Loretta Lynn are all included in Amberley Beatty's assortment of tributes. The Fusion Talent Group noted that she "is one of the most diverse and sought-after tribute artists in North

You Sound Just Like…

Amberley Beatty fell in love with Patsy Cline and her music because of the emotion in Cline's singing: "She could make you feel the simplest of songs." When Beatty discovered that she shared a similar tone, she started incorporating Cline's tunes into her repertoire (courtesy Amberley Beatty).

America."[10] Her attention to detail and authenticity transports audiences back in time. In 2010, Beatty enjoyed solo success with "If I Could Spend Today Loving You," sung with Allen Karl. It was a Top Ten hit on the European Indie charts.

Amberley Beatty was born on August 31, 1978, in Kitchener, Ontario, Canada. At two years old, she sang along with all the TV commercials. Beatty revealed, "After that, I was obsessed with 'You Are My Sunshine,' and when I was four, I was at a Christmas party with my mom and dad when they got me up to sing that song."[11] When she was a young girl, her stepfather got into a bad accident and almost died, and she lived with her grandparents for four months while he recuperated: "They were old-fashioned farmers, so every morning we sat at the breakfast table and listened to the local country radio station. I heard Conway Twitty, Patsy Cline, George Jones, Hank Williams [Sr.], Loretta Lynn and many more. I especially fell in love with the human emotion in everything that Patsy sang. She could make you feel the simplest of songs, and I listened to her every nuance. My grandpa would sing along,

Five. Women Who Rock

and I would copy him as he was my idol. I believe that music just called to my soul. I love the timeline of the '50s and '60s, its beauty in simplicity, and its complexity in terms of women—how they were identified in the world and their struggles. I've been called an old soul many times, and I truly believe that I was born in the wrong time."

At 15, Beatty was the lead in school plays. Four years later, she appeared in *Oliver* and *Anne of Green Gables* at Kitchener's Centre in the Square. She admitted, "I was an introvert and quite shy. It gave me a way to share with people. During this time, I also found that I had a similar tone to Patsy's, so I kept singing." Some of her favorite singers are Cline, Madonna, Loretta Lynn, Aerosmith, Bryan Adams, Bruce Springsteen, George Jones and Bonnie Tyler.

After high school, Beatty continued with community theater and loved every minute. Eventually, she got married, had kids and opened a hair salon, which made it too difficult to continue with theater since it entailed spending three months in rehearsals and shows. She turned to karaoke as an outlet: "A table full of regulars soon invited me into their group, and it became a weekly thing. One of the regulars was Shon Carroll, an Elvis Tribute Artist, who had lost his son in a house fire and was fundraising to help fire prevention. He asked me to be a part of it. I was flattered and shocked. I asked what I should sing, and he said, 'Some Patsy and a Loretta song or two.' I chose 'Crazy' by Patsy, 'Coal Miner's Daughter' by Loretta, then some Dixie Chicks and Evanescence. As soon as I finished, Shon said I should do this [regularly]."

A year later, Beatty performed as Cline at an Elvis birthday bash. She sewed her own outfit, which included a bolero jacket, and bought cowboy boots (which she spray-painted white) from a thrift store. She did her own hair and makeup to make the transformation complete: "I was both scared and exhilarated, but I felt like it was where I was supposed to be. Then, for a few years, I only did a handful of Patsy shows, here and there, for Shon and others who were putting on Elvis events."

An agent presented her with the chance to portray Connie Francis: "He called and asked if I did Connie, and I said, 'No, I do not.' He said, 'Well, would you please give it a try because I believe you have the right tone and think you could do it.' I practiced for about three months and did my first show with only five songs. Her personality was so different from Patsy's that it was kind of neat to take on that character." In November 2018, Beatty was scheduled to perform in Florida at Francis' book signing, but she was unable to attend because of a car accident: "The idea literally scared the crap out of me because I would have wanted to make her proud with my tribute."

Beatty typically tours in Canada, although she has done a few performances in the U.S. and Mexico. She has her own band, and the shows are 90 minutes in length. Beatty always includes the hits but also poignant ones: "I make sure that there's a flow to the set—one song must go into the next." Her favorites to sing as Cline are "Always" and "Tennessee Waltz"; as Lynn, "Success" and "Somebody Somewhere (Don't Know What He's Missin' Tonight)"; and as Francis, "Fallin'" and "I'm Sorry I Made You Cry." On occasion, Beatty has been asked to sing a song that she doesn't know: "I go backstage, and while putting on my makeup, I learn it. If the band doesn't know it, then I sing it *a cappella*. If they do, then we get through it best we can." Beatty's most embarrassing moment came while she was waiting to do her second set as Cline at a Montreal theater: "I had only sung a song and a half, then the power went out in the entire building. Thanks to the light on my phone, I walked down the stairs and asked the crowd to sing with me while the piano player played some chords on his iPad. In the dark, I managed to finish my set somehow."

Besides her tribute shows, Beatty has also showcased her individual talent: "I taught myself a few chords on the guitar, enough to write some songs. I had always written poems that were quite lyrical in terms of music. I had these things stuck in my head but had no idea how to get them onto paper. In 2008, a lovely man named Allen Karl found me on the Internet, called me, and asked if I'd come to Nashville, all expenses paid, to record an album. At 17, he had sung with Patsy on 'As Far as I'm Concerned.' We were going to do an album of his songs along with that cover and a few others." In 2010, that album, *If I Could Spend Today Loving You*, was released on Century II Records.

Beatty even got to share the stage with Gene Watson once: "He's such a huge artist, so that was a thrill." She added, "I'm very proud of my independent music." As for her tributes, "I'm extremely grateful to be able to spread the joy that I have felt from this music. It truly makes me happy to be able to help keep alive the greatest women in music because they deserve to be remembered and celebrated."

Elaine Wesley (Patsy Cline)

Elaine Wesley began her professional singing career in 1974, but it wasn't until she married Garry Wesley that she added Patsy Cline to her repertoire. Since 1988, the Wesleys have performed together at theaters, casinos, arenas, large festivals and churches throughout the U.S., Canada and Mexico. Garry pays tribute to Elvis Presley, primarily the 1970s jumpsuit era. They often incorporate a few duets into their sets, such as "Pledging My Love" and "Let It Be Me."

Elaine came from a musical background: "My parents were both singers, and my father played guitar and wrote his own songs."[12] At ten years old, she sang for the first time on stage with her father. The tune was "I Can't Stop Thinking of You." Her parents were the biggest supporters of her dreams and her main musical influences. Patsy Cline and Tammy Wynette were also influences. Her favorite singers included Elvis, Connie Francis, Brenda Lee, Trisha Yearwood and Reba McEntire.

On December 31, 1988, she first showcased her tribute to Cline. She could have chosen another female act, such as Loretta Lynn or June Carter, but Cline stood out. Wesley revealed, "I love her hits. It reflects the emotions she felt when they were recorded and, in many ways, some of the same emotions I have felt in the past. I sang with Patsy whenever I rehearsed, so I could try and copy the reflections in her voice." Her favorites to sing are "Crazy," "I Fall to Pieces," "So Wrong" and "Sweet Dreams." When Wesley gets a request for a song she doesn't know, she acknowledges that fact, then sings one that she does know. As part of her husband's show, her portion is 40 minutes.

Her most memorable experiences have been appearances on Nashville's *You Can Be a Star* and performances with

On March 5, 1997, Elaine Wesley shared the stage for the first time with The Jordanaires (courtesy Elaine Wesley).

You Sound Just Like...

The Jordanaires: "On March 5, 1997, I sang for the first time with them in Mississippi. A small man wearing a golf cap, who was sitting in the audience, waved at me during soundcheck. I simply waved back, not knowing it was Gordon Stoker of The Jordanaires."

Besides paying homage to Cline, Wesley is a gifted songwriter, having penned over 200 tunes. She acknowledged, "Lyrics always come first and are usually due to a personal experience or heartache because that's the nature of good country music. I recorded my first single in Nashville in 1983 after winning Wisconsin Country Band of the Year."

Six

"Hello, I'm Johnny Cash"

Zach McNabb

There are tribute artists who go the whole nine yards in their portrayal where they dress the part, talk and sing like the legendary act, and adopt the singer's mannerisms. One might refer to them as

In preparation for his first album release, Zach McNabb teamed up with Carl Sonny Leyland. Jon Atkinson, the owner of Bigtone Records, had Leyland listen to a few of McNabb's previous recordings. Leyland became a fan and decided that he wanted to play piano on McNabb's session recordings and provide some of his own rockabilly songs (photograph by Travis Stevenson; courtesy Zach McNabb).

You Sound Just Like...

impersonators. Others are strictly giving homage to the country and rockabilly songbooks. Young Zach McNabb is a singer who honors his roots, paying particular attention to the music of Johnny Cash, Hank Williams Sr., Ernest Tubb, Hawkshaw Hawkins and Hank Thompson, as well as Elvis Presley's early recordings on the Sun and RCA record labels. He acknowledged, "My vocals are often compared to [those of] Johnny and Hank, which is a wonderful compliment to receive and sure does make me feel great."[1]

McNabb was born on September 27, 2002, in Johnson City, Tennessee. His mother introduced him to '50s music: "She would turn on the oldies, and we would dance in our living room together, along with my other siblings. Then, when I was 13, I really got interested and began listening to a lot of songs and artists that I remembered from when I was younger, such as 'Rock Around the Clock,' 'All Shook Up,' 'Everyday,' 'Splish Splash' and 'Dream Lover.'" His musical influences are mostly represented in classic country with the likes of Cash, Williams, Tubb, Hawkins, Thompson and Bill Monroe.

In 2010, McNabb took guitar lessons at Trinity Arts Center in Johnson City. He then put the instrument down for a few years: "After picking it up again at age 13, I began taking lessons from Art Gibson, who played guitar in the worship band at my church. I learned from him for a year or two, and then I began teaching myself. Today, I still primarily teach myself; however, I do take lessons occasionally." When McNabb was 14, he began singing; one of his first tunes was "Folsom Prison Blues." In August 2021, he decided to further expand his musical knowledge by enrolling in the entertainment technology program at Northeast State Community College in Blountville, Tennessee. He will study copyright, managing live sound, and running lights. McNabb is also taking a course in recording engineering, which teaches students the different types of microphones, various recording techniques, and how to use a digital workstation for mixing. McNabb admitted, "I'm so glad I found this program. I'm excited as it's the perfect fit for me. In the future, I can potentially work for a studio or lighting and sound company in Nashville."

From July 2018 until February 2021, his band, Zach McNabb and the Tennessee Esquires, featured McNabb on vocals and rhythm guitar, his younger brother Caleb on doghouse bass and fiddle, and Willie Vance on lead guitar. They had their first gig on a sidewalk in front of a "farmers' market" in downtown Erwin, Tennessee. "Willie and I met through my grandma and his aunt. My grandma told his aunt how I

Six. "Hello, I'm Johnny Cash"

played guitar, sang, and liked Elvis Presley and Johnny Cash. Then his aunt told my grandma that her nephew liked the same things. His aunt told him he should contact me. Willie and I began to talk and really hit it off, so I invited him over to my great grandma's house that Sunday, where all my family eats lunch after church. Willie came over, and we played Johnny Cash and early Elvis songs and talked for hours." Vance was soon playing guitar in the band. After nearly three years, Vance quit so he could spend more time with his family and focus on his day job. McNabb revealed, "We're still looking for somebody to fill his spot, full-time."

Incidentally, several names were considered before they settled on Zach McNabb and the Tennessee Esquires: "We always liked the band names—Elvis Presley and the Blue Moon Boys, Johnny Cash and the Tennessee Two, Buddy Holly and the Crickets, Ernest Tubb and his Texas Troubadours, but the one that stuck out the most was Johnny Cash and the Tennessee Two because we are from Tennessee. We didn't want to call ourselves Zach McNabb and the Tennessee Two, though, since that would basically be stealing their name; we wanted to be more original. We began to think some more, and Willie brought up the word *esquire* because of his love for the Esquire guitar that Fender built in the '50s. It was one of the guitars that Luther Perkins played early in his career. We then searched for the word's definition, and in Britain, *esquire* is applied to a commoner who has gained the social position of a gentleman, or a young nobleman in training for knighthood." They liked that, and became Zach McNabb and the Tennessee Esquires.

Their regular gigs include the Boones Creek Museum and Opry and the Jonesborough Barrel House, both in Tennessee. During July 2021, McNabb and his brother performed every weekend at Smoky Mountains Tunes and Tales in Gatlinburg, Tennessee: "We played up and down the street to all the people passing by. That was so much fun." Typically, their shows last an hour, but if someone requests an extended performance, they will oblige. McNabb revealed, "The songs I always include in my shows are 'That's All Right,' 'Folsom Prison Blues,' 'Blue Moon of Kentucky,' 'The Wreck of Old' 97,' 'Get Rhythm' and 'Blue Suede Shoes.'" McNabb also enjoys singing gospel tunes such as "I Was There When It Happened," "I Saw the Light" and "Where the Soul of Man Never Dies," because "it gives me a way to be a witness for God, a way to give Him the glory, and to thank Him for the talent and opportunities that He has blessed me with." On one occasion, they received a request for "Hound Dog," and McNabb knew the lyrics, but they had never played the song together: "It wasn't too bad for the first time. Everyone really enjoyed it. We have [since] worked on it some more and have added it to our set."

In early 2019, McNabb began work on his first album at Bigtone Records in Bristol, Virginia. He revealed, "One day, Jon Atkinson, owner of Bigtone Records, and I were talking, and he said that he let Carl Sonny Leyland listen to some of my recordings. He told me that Carl really liked my voice and style and that he had some original songs he had written that I could record if I was interested. I told Jon that I was, and he said that Carl would be coming to Bristol for a week at the end of August, beginning of September, to do multiple sessions with different musicians. On September 2, my brother and I went over [to the studio] with our parents and met Carl, Dean Shot and Devin Neel for the first time. We recorded four fantastic rockabilly–rock and roll songs that Carl had written, on all vintage equipment, in only two or three takes. Carl played piano; Dean played lead guitar; Devin played drums, while my brother Caleb played upright bass, and I sang and played rhythm guitar. I really enjoyed working with Carl. I love him. He's a really nice guy. We still have a lot of work to do to make it a full album, and Carl's not sure when he's coming back. Therefore, soon, we are leaning toward the release of an EP."

McNabb feels very fortunate that he has parents who are highly supportive of his musical endeavors: "They have always encouraged my brothers and me in our music, taking us to lessons and gigs. They are my biggest fans."

He revealed, "My current focus is to move more into the country scene. I just feel I'll be able to get a lot more opportunities, especially in the area I live in. My voice and style are more in the direction of country and bluegrass, but I'll still do rockabilly. That music is so good that it's hard not to [want to sing it]. My favorite aspect of performing is being on stage doing something I love with my brother Caleb. I also enjoy putting smiles on people's faces. I really enjoy entertaining, and I hope it's something I can always do."

Pete Storm

For two years, Pete Storm, who hails from the United Kingdom, concentrated his efforts on competing in Elvis Tribute Artist competitions, hoping to win as many as possible. He participated in the Ultimate in Memphis twice and placed third both times. In 2011, he won

Six. "Hello, I'm Johnny Cash"

first prize at the Images of the King, the Collingwood Elvis Festival and the European Masters. These accolades made him one of the world's top ETAs. Storm stated, "I eventually retired from competitions because they were too nerve-wracking."[2] Even though he halted his involvement with the contests, Storm continued to impress Presley fans worldwide with his live performances: "Elvis is a big deal all over the world, and it never ceases to amaze me. The largest crowd I played to was probably the Elvis Days Festival in Italy. It was an outdoor event, and there were people for as far as I could see. It was amazing, and I felt like the real Elvis up there, on that stage." In 2018, he had to discontinue his tribute to Presley because of voice problems. However, he is grateful that he can still perform as Johnny Cash: "[His voice] is in a much lower register, so it makes [his songs] easier to sing."

Storm's adoration for Presley began as a small child: "I was always drawn to Elvis' songs on the radio, and I loved his movies on TV." When he was almost six, his mother recorded him singing "Mean Woman Blues." His first Elvis Presley gig, he arranged himself: "I rented out my local soccer club's function room and sold tickets. I borrowed my

Pete Storm grew up listening to Elvis Presley's songs on the radio and watching his movies on TV. He was five when his mother recorded him singing "Mean Woman Blues." These days, Storm does a tribute to Johnny Cash (courtesy Pete Storm).

You Sound Just Like...

friend's homemade jumpsuit, rented a PA and bought some backing tracks. I was so nervous, and my mum thought I was crazy, but it was a great success." In 2005, he decided to pursue the possibility of becoming an Elvis Tribute Artist after he sang karaoke at a bar; the owner was so impressed that he hired him on the spot. Eventually, both Storm's mom and dad embraced his vocation and, to this day, are very proud of his tributes.

For five years, Storm honed his act and developed his fan base at various European venues. Theaters, festivals, and cruise ships welcomed him with open arms. In January 2010, he made the finals in the European Elvis Championships, his first competition ever. From then on, his popularity soared and he toured the world—Australia, the Far East and America. He recalled an embarrassing moment he once had as an ETA: "I split my pants. I tried a high kick and felt them go. Luckily, it was near the end of the show, so I just faced the crowd for the last few songs."

In his shows, Storm concentrated on material from Presley's 1970s catalogue. His favorites to sing were the ballads, such as "Separate Ways" and "I Miss You." However, he always felt it was a little self-indulgent to include too many in a set: "The casual fans just wanted the hits, really, so I couldn't do a set without including 'Suspicious Minds' and 'Can't Help Falling in Love.' If I ever forgot the lyrics, I tried to bluff my way through or was just honest and owned up to it, then I'd ask the audience to help me." He paid particular attention to detail on how he looked: "I have replicas of all the suits from [the film] *That's the Way It Is*, but my favorite jumpsuit will always be the Concho. It is just perfection."

These days, Storm is strictly a Johnny Cash tribute artist. His favorites to sing are "Big River" and "Ghost Riders in the Sky." He admitted, "I've always loved the honesty of Johnny Cash's records. To me, it's like listening to the truth. I became more of a fan of Johnny's after I heard his cover of the Nine Inch Nails song 'Hurt.' The video always moves me as it's very emotional. I loved how Johnny became popular again in the '90s with [his series of albums] *The American Recordings*. He was a truly great man with an unmistakable voice." He often participates in *Sun Records: The Concert*, a famous theatrical production in the United Kingdom. Both Sun Records and the Johnny Cash Estate have endorsed this musical.

Storm lists Presley and Cash as inspirations along with Neil Diamond, Dean Martin ("he had so much charisma and was hilarious") and Frank Sinatra.

Six. "Hello, I'm Johnny Cash"

Christopher Essex

The musical *Million Dollar Quartet* began as a one-month production in Florida in the winter of 2006. A short time later, it received thunderous praise for its incarnations in Chicago and New York City. While it was on Broadway, Levi Kreis won a Tony for his portrayal of Jerry Lee Lewis. Fifteen years later, and *Million Dollar Quartet* is still going strong.

For two years, Christopher Essex portrayed Johnny Cash in the stage show: "I appeared in almost 200 shows. I can honestly say that every time I stepped on stage as Johnny, I felt so overwhelmingly grateful for the opportunities that he and the show offered me."[3] In December 2019, Essex left the theater world behind and moved to Nashville to pursue his dream of becoming a country singer. In October 2020, he released his debut single, "Swipe Right on Me."

Essex grew up with his single mom and no siblings. His love for country music began at an early age, listening to the radio with his mom and hearing many of the country legends. The newer country music also had a major influence on him. Essex enjoyed rockabilly and '50s and '60s rock as well. He doesn't remember a time when he didn't sing. In the first grade, he was a member of the choir. His first exposure to musical theater came when he was six: "My mom and I went to see *The Music Man*. She said that when '76 Trombones' started to play, I marched down the aisle and sang along." That love for the stage continued, and in the third grade, he auditioned for a role in *Annie Get Your Gun*. Essex recalled, "I've always felt most comfortable on a stage. I was bullied a lot growing up."[4]

During his junior year in college, he taught himself how to play the guitar, so he could send in an audition tape for *Million Dollar Quartet*: "I had gone to a unified audition, which is where you go and slate yourself for several summer stock theaters that review your work and call you back if interested. I received a call back from a theater in Macon, Missouri, for *Million Dollar Quartet*. They asked if I was familiar with Johnny Cash. I was raised on country music, so I most certainly was. They then asked if I played guitar. I didn't but responded, 'I'm not the best.' They asked me to record any Johnny Cash song and send a video their way. I ordered a cheap practice guitar, went online and taught myself 'Ring of Fire.'" He practiced that song for three hours every day for a week: "I did the whole song with two-finger picking because I couldn't hold the pick. I messed up a couple chords, but I basically sent

You Sound Just Like...

a message saying, 'Y'all don't know me, but I see that this show could be something for me, and I think I'm right for this. I promise you, by the time it's day one of rehearsals, I'll know everything."[5] He got the job from that audition. He had to learn 27 songs in just a few months. Essex

When Christopher Essex submitted an audition tape for *Million Dollar Quartet,* he sang Johnny Cash's "Ring of Fire." He had to learn how to play guitar in only a week. Winning the role in that musical was a life-changing experience: "Guitar has become so much a part of who I am that I can't remember how life was before" (courtesy Christopher Essex).

made sure to thoroughly study Johnny Cash, to learn as much about him as he could. That research paid off as he was hired consistently for two years to play the Man in Black.

In 2018, Essex graduated with a Bachelor of Fine Arts degree in theater from Carnegie Mellon University in Pittsburgh. He acknowledged, "I'd say my theater background has helped me build my vocal stamina. When you have to do a show like *Million Dollar Quartet* eight times a week, it takes strictly regimented warm-ups and vocal techniques." That same year, he released *Country State of Mind*: "It was comprised of all cover songs that I felt had impactful stories. For this reason, it was an ultra–low-budget attempt to see what being a recording artist was like and how much prep work goes into studio time. I used digital equipment, and two of the tracks, 'Your Man' and 'Come Over,' were pulled from live shows."

Essex's mother had always wished that her son would become a country singer. In December 2019, he took a significant step toward making her dream a reality when he moved to Nashville to begin a recording career. A tornado damaged his home three months after the move, and then the coronavirus pandemic hampered any plans to record or play live. Even though he had thoughts of moving back to Florida, he remained in Nashville and turned his struggles into songs. His debut release, "Swipe Right on Me," was inspired by a traffic light stop. It was there that he had been perusing the dating app Tinder. Since Essex was new in town, he was looking to meet someone, to go out dancing. He took that idea and wrote the song with Bill DiLuigi. It's a line dance tune with a rockabilly feel. It owes some gratitude to Carl Perkins' "Matchbox," since that was the song that Essex was playing when he came up with the lyrics for "Swipe Right on Me."

Essex explained his typical songwriting process: "I'll often start by creating a chord progression with a melody line. Then I'll write a rough sketch of a poem. I'll start to sing through those lines, do some editing and expanding, and after a while, I have a song." An EP consisting of all original material was issued at the end of 2021, and Essex hopes to showcase the new songs for his supporters soon. One of his most ardent admirers is his mom: "She tries to come to every single show. She's amazingly supportive, and I am so grateful for her." A mantra that he learned while earning a black belt in karate was "Goals we set are goals we get." He stated, "This phrase has continually shaped my life and helped guide me to where I am today."

Seven

"Walk a Mile in My Shoes"
1970s Elvis

Leo Days

Tribute artists pay particular attention to nuances when it comes to the vocals and movements of the performers they portray. Some go the extra mile, like Leo Days, and study every detail, including the icon's mannerisms. He acknowledged that he is also an ace at remembering lyrics: "I'm terrible with names, but I know songs word for word that I haven't heard in 10 or 15 years. Once I know a song, I never forget it."[1] He's also one of the few Elvis Tribute Artists who portrays all three eras of Presley in one show.

Days was born on October 3, 1980, in Honolulu, Hawaii, and became an instant Presley fan three years later: "I thought Elvis was the coolest thing I had ever seen."[2]

He continued, "I always liked Elvis' music. My dad was a huge Elvis fan, as was his mom before him, so his music was always around. As early as age three, I would memorize entire Elvis movies and perform them at family reunions. I didn't know I was preparing for a 'role.' I was just a kid, having fun."

Days has been singing for as long as he can remember: "In my early teens, I used to sing for my friends. The first time I sang an Elvis song was in my parents' basement on a karaoke machine they had bought. The song was 'Separate Ways.' I decided to try and make my voice sound like his. My mom came running downstairs and asked if that was me singing. I looked around and said, 'There's nobody else down here, Mom.' I was only 14 or 15 at the time, and the only places around here that had karaoke were bars. I had an uncle who was a policeman, and he would call ahead to make sure I could get in." Due to his age, Days could only stay at the bars until nine p.m. "My uncle then took me to an Eagles' Club and I sang 'The Wonder of You.' I got

Seven. "Walk a Mile in My Shoes"

quite a reaction. People started coming up to me and asking if I did shows. I had no idea what that meant but knew I was on to something."

A short time later, he participated in a talent contest at the Genesee County Fair in Mount Morris, Michigan: "I had bought an awful wig and a Halloween costume jumpsuit. I sang 'Moody Blue' in the first round and 'Viva Las Vegas' in the second. I won. The prize was $1000 and a $200 savings bond. Minutes after winning, I was put onto a golf cart and taken over to the main stage to open for a country act named Clay Walker in front of 10,000 people. I was only 15 years old and had never seen

In 2019, Leo Days made a triumphant return to the Michigan Elvis Festival in Ypsilanti, Michigan. He has been in it off and on for 20 years, and gets to reunite with a lot of his loyal fans each time (courtesy Leo Days).

that many people before." (The talent contest only had 20 people in attendance.)

He revealed, "I was scared to death, and it felt like an eternity before my music finally started. After performing my song, the people in charge of entertainment at the fair asked me to do two 90-minute performances over the next two days. I agreed, went straight home, and did the best I could to get the music together for those performances."

For the next ten years, Days performed locally at theaters and fairs until he signed with Rock and Roll Inc. in Los Angeles. Then he traveled nationally with the show *Three Faces of the King*. In 2009, he joined *Legends in Concert*: "In 2008, I had placed in the Top Five in the Ultimate [Elvis Tribute Artists Contest], and a representative from *Legends* saw me and booked me the following summer at Foxwoods [Resort Casino in Mashantucket, Connecticut]. I have performed for the *Legends* venues in Hawaii, Myrtle Beach, Branson, Las Vegas, Foxwoods, Foley, Alabama and aboard the *Norwegian Epic* and *Norwegian Pearl* cruise ships. I primarily do *Legends in Concert* shows, and they are usually only a 20-minute set. When I do my own, a couple of times a year, the show runs around two hours with intermission." The Michigan Elvis Festival in Ypsilanti, Michigan, is one of the venues he has played often. He's performed on its stage off and on for the past 20 years. "I love it there. It's fun to hang out with the other ETAs and see a lot of the familiar [fan] faces who have supported me. The first time I played there, I was only 18, and the festival brought in about 12,000 people. That was quite a rush, considering how the people fought over scarves and grabbed at me. It was the first time I ever had the feeling of what it was like for Elvis."

Days said that a lot of factors come into play as he prepares his setlists: "It depends on the length of the performance, the venue and the type of audience. I always try and include many of the hits. For an Elvis festival, I get to do some obscure songs, which is always fun. My favorite tune of Elvis' to sing changes almost daily. Elvis has so many different types of songs. I will say it is almost always a ballad. Today, it's 'Surrender.' My favorite era of Elvis to perform is definitely 1969, 1970. I loved the amount of energy he put into his show during the early Vegas performances."

Similar to Presley, Days can also play the guitar and the piano: "I started playing guitar at [the age of] 16. The same uncle who took me to karaoke showed me a few chords. The first song I learned to play was 'That's All Right.' I didn't start playing piano until I was 23. I took a few lessons and learned to play 'You'll Never Walk Alone.'"

Seven. "Walk a Mile in My Shoes"

Days didn't realize that he could make a living as a tribute artist until he was actually doing it. He tried to convince his mother that she should make some extra money as a seamstress, but she wasn't interested. Although, she did construct all of Days' costumes until he was 25. She was so good that other ETAs wanted her to sew for them, but she refused. Her son would be her only client. Days revealed, "I still have one outfit that she made, and it has been altered should I decide to ever wear it again."

His portrayal of Presley has occupied the majority of his career, but in recent years he's added Michael Jackson to his repertoire. Days explained, "I had been portraying Elvis for about 15 years and wanted to try something new. There was a Michael Jackson in the *Legends* show I was in at the time, in Hawaii, and I watched his set. It looked like a lot of fun, so I asked him to show me how to do the makeup and a few basic principles of some of the dance moves. I never in my wildest dreams thought of doing a tribute show to him because I didn't look like that. After I found out that makeup could change that, I really went to work and studied for hours on end. Michael was my generation's Elvis, so I was a huge fan growing up. I remember watching the first time he moonwalked on *Motown 25*. In fact, watching some of his performances in the early '80s inspired me to want to be a performer in the first place. My first gig as Michael was at a club in Arizona. The footage, with the exception of the opening song because the audio was too bad, is on my YouTube page. I was really nervous, but it went over very well."

One of Days' proudest moments was being selected to play Presley in Cirque du Soleil's production *Viva Elvis*, which premiered at the Aria Hotel in Las Vegas on February 19, 2010: "I sent my video to the production staff at Cirque du Soleil and got the part. I don't know how or why, and I never asked. Working for *Viva Elvis* was one of the wildest experiences of my life. Everywhere you looked, there was somebody doing something amazing. If you looked right, guys were flipping through the air on trampolines, and then if you looked left, acrobats were doing flips. It was jaw-dropping. I got to work side by side with director Vincent Paterson, who won multiple Tony Awards and worked with Michael Jackson and Madonna. Priscilla Presley even saw me dance in one of the numbers. I also sang 'Blue Suede Shoes' acoustically with the band while she watched. It was quite intimidating, to say the least. I was in production with them for six months, but they cut my part two weeks before the opening. …Being surrounded by talent at that level was an experience that I'll never forget."

You Sound Just Like...

Doug Church

Dubbed "The True Voice of Elvis" by fellow Elvis Tribute Artists and some of Presley's confidants, Doug Church began his singing career in 1983 while serving in the U.S. Air Force. During four years of enlistment, he competed in numerous talent contests and racked up 11 first-place trophies. A short time later, he won his first ETA competition in Memphis. More accolades followed, including his 2003 induction into the Elvis Tribute Artists Hall of Fame and, in 2014, a Heart of the King Lifetime Achievement Award.

Church also has a rare distinction in the ETA world: He is an ordained minister. If a couple chooses, he can marry them dressed as Elvis Presley.

At age ten, Church was singing harmonies with his brothers in their gospel quartet. In 1976, while he was attending junior high, a fellow student introduced him to Presley's music via his 45 RPM record collection: "They were mostly movie songs. We then developed a healthy competition between us to see who could sound the most like Elvis. I sang (with just my guitar) to the girls in hopes of winning their hearts. It was effective to some degree. Not sure what the songs were, but I can guess they were most likely ballads like 'Love Me Tender.' From there, it turned into a love affair with what I call the best music in the world; music which speaks to any situation, any emotion you can conceive, and got me through many rough times in my life. Elvis' music was so happy and uplifting that I couldn't help but gravitate toward it.[3]

"However, back then, I had no aspirations of becoming a singer or an ETA. Until I heard Jimmy Ellis, aka Orion, Ronnie McDowell or Alan Meyer, I had no idea there was such a thing as professional ETAs. They were my inspirations, and I've had the pleasure of working side by side with one of them, Mr. Ronnie McDowell. It's not often one gets to meet their hero, work with them, and even have them compliment you in front of the audience." Church was also influenced by Elton John, Ray Charles, The Blues Brothers, Kiss, Led Zeppelin, Queen, Meatloaf, and the Three Tenors.

In 1983, Church enlisted in the Air Force and was made a security policeman. The Air Force held annual talent contests, and a G.I. dared Church to compete. At the time, he was stationed at RAF Bentwaters in the U.K.: "Wearing a homemade costume and painted-on sideburns, I played guitar and sang two songs, 'Love Me' and 'Love Me Tender.' I won first place in my category, which was musical potpourri, and went on to

Seven. "Walk a Mile in My Shoes"

higher levels of competition." Church competed on the local level, then moved on to regional contests where he traveled to various military bases across Europe. Everywhere Church went, he trounced the other contestants: "I was competing against dozens of other acts in different categories, ranging anywhere from male vocalist to comedian to musical groups. I think, because the loss of Elvis was so recent, people were clamoring for more of his music, which served me well in the long run." By the time his four years were up, Church had won 11 first place trophies. He was going to re-enlist, but changed his plans when Uncle Sam promised bonus checks to those who decided to opt out of the military.

Civilian life provided him more opportunities to hone his Presley tribute. He recalled, "My first paying gig as Elvis was a Christmas show in a shopping mall. I wore a pair of denim jeans, split from knee to ankle, with a kick pleat sewn in to simulate a jumpsuit, and a black leather jacket. It was hideous." Thereafter, he rented jumpsuits from costume shops until he could find an adequate seamstress. He added, "After the show, I'll never forget a little old lady came up to me and said, 'You ain't no Elvis!' Not being able to think of anything clever to say, I simply blurted out, 'No, ma'am. Elvis is dead.' The overall reaction to the show was one of playful appreciation

Doug Church's first paying gig as Elvis was at a shopping mall. After the show, one older lady approached him and blurted out, "You ain't no Elvis." He comically quipped back, "No ma'am, Elvis is dead" (photograph by Eva Brand; courtesy Doug Church).

and novel interest because I don't think there were any ETAs in my area yet." Church managed a car wash and laundromat while moonlighting as an ETA.

In the late '80s, Church recorded a tape of his vocal talents. The technician running the tape machine was so impressed that he lined up a gig for Church. He was hired to perform a few love songs to backing tracks for a couple's anniversary. Church found success performing in nightclubs, but his fan base grew once he attended Memphis contests. He also then discovered that there were other ETAs in the world: "What an eye-opening experience to know you're not the only ETA around. In my first attempt, I won second place, but I took the videotape back home to study." The following year, 1991, he entered the competition held at Bad Bob Vapors in Memphis: "I sang 'An American Trilogy,' 'My Way' and 'Hurt' and won. The prize was $500 and a huge trophy, one of my most prized possessions. I had competed against 15 or 20 other guys from all over the world."

Two years later, Church started working for *Legends in Concert* in Las Vegas: "I auditioned and was told by John Stewart, the producer-creator, that he thought I had a great voice but was too heavy and that I needed to go home and lose ten pounds. Well, I worked hard, lost 15 pounds, and a few weeks later came back to Vegas and auditioned again. John looked at me and said, 'That's it.' That night, he put me on the stage. It is a good thing I had thought ahead and brought my jumpsuit with me. After that, I performed for [many of the] *Legends*—in Vegas, Laughlin, Nevada; Myrtle Beach, South Carolina; Branson, Missouri; Bangkok, Hong Kong, and Moscow. It was a great seven years, but I had had enough of singing the same damn five songs over and over. It was two shows a night, six days a week. I was beginning to lose my chops, so to speak. I decided to get my own shows together and tour the country."

Mostly theaters, primarily on the East Coast, showcase his talent. "I also do banquet halls and private functions for around 200 people. My shows are anywhere from 74 minutes to two 40-minute sets, with an intermission." Mainly for financial reasons, Church does half of his performances with a live band, Kentucky Reign, while on the others, he uses backing tracks. "The largest crowds I have are at major sporting events. For the Chicago White Sox, I sang for the audience outside the park before the game—two 40-minute sets. Then I came in and sang the National Anthem. During the seventh-inning stretch, I got back into my costume and did four songs right on the field." One of his more popular shows is *Beyond 77,* "which is a what-if concept revolving around the premise that Elvis would've canceled his last remaining shows in August of '77 and checked himself into Baptist Memorial Hospital for rest and relaxation. Having taken some time to get his life back on track, he lays low for about six years, then decides he must have a second comeback with a new look, sound and players."

Church fills the majority of his setlists with audience suggestions that he has received via email: "I have a basic outline and just fill in the rest with what the people want to hear. You gotta have your opener, 'C.C. Rider,' and your closer—most often 'Can't Help Falling in Love,' but the rest belong to the people. Once I sang 'Oh Holy Night,' which had been requested, *a cappella*, and it became a staple in my shows from then on. Gospel music is by far my favorite because it's comforting and reassuring [to know] that there's somebody bigger than you and I, and there's more to life than one's own little bubble."

Church's shows usually come off without a hitch, but he has had a few pratfalls: "I once had my jumpsuit split onstage. I was a bit heavier at the time, and when I knelt to give a scarf, a loud pop occurred. I blew out the leg of that jumpsuit from inner thigh to knee. Fortunately, nothing was exposed [due to the] lining of the suit, but needless to say, I had to go make a quick change before the show could continue. On that same show, I was using a band that was pantomiming to my tracks because the band I had backed out at the last minute. With no one the wiser, we were pulling it off until one of my tracks decided to skip numerous times. The promoter came on stage and announced the nature of our malfunction, and the audience had a good laugh about it. I was mortified that we'd been found out."

Comedy is frequently incorporated into his act, thanks to his ability to do character voices, over 50 different ones in fact: "As a kid, I spent a lot of time alone, watching television and trying to mimic the voices I enjoyed most—Richard Nixon, The Muppets and Rodney Dangerfield. The list of voices has changed over the years; some have dropped off while others have been added due to their current popularity. Once in a while, I'll throw into the show my favorite character voice, Redd Foxx, aka Fred G. Sanford, in a song called 'Seven Spanish Angels,' which initially featured Ray Charles and Willie Nelson. However, Ray is replaced by Elvis; I can do a fair Willie Nelson. At the end of the song, I introduce the third member, Fred Sanford, and the crowd goes insane."

Church is continuously implementing new ideas to give his performances a fresh approach. He even assists his "brothers" in the ETA world by instructing them in the training series *Sing Like the King*. It covers every aspect that an ETA needs to perfect his stage act: vocals, mannerisms, dance moves, wardrobe, hair, etc. As Bruce Springsteen has famously said, "There have been pretenders, and there have been contenders, but there is only one king."[4] Church knows he's not Presley: "I perform each and every show as a tribute, and out of respect for the King. You really can't impersonate the greatest legend of all time."[5]

Michael St. Angel

Michael St. Angel wasn't a big Elvis Presley fan growing up, although he did enjoy oldies music. Therefore, to prepare for the role, he dove in by watching footage from Presley's concerts and listening to his songs, and trying to absorb as much as possible: "My appreciation for Elvis is mostly centered on his musical catalogue, his recording sessions, and what he brought to the stage in his live performances. Elvis was a flawed human being, just like the rest of us, but he was gifted with tremendous talent, and he was the greatest entertainer to have ever

Michael St. Angel relates more to Elvis' 1970s jumpsuit era. His favorite songs to perform are "Suspicious Minds," "An American Trilogy," "My Way" and "Little Darlin'" (courtesy Michael St. Angel).

lived. I did plenty of research, and one person who initially had loads of advice for me was Art Kistler. He was a really valuable resource and was always eager to give guidance on sound equipment, wardrobe, singing techniques, and more. He's a super guy, and we've remained friends."[6]

It was in 2004 that St. Angel decided to become an Elvis Tribute Artist. Before that, he hadn't sung much: "I do recall singing karaoke in a local bar, and some girl approached me and said I sounded just like Chris Isaak. That was my initial tiptoeing into this world, and things quickly evolved from there."

He added, "I can't say for certain why I gravitated toward Elvis specifically, but at the time it made sense for some reason, and it was a great challenge for me to see if I could succeed as an ETA since outside of a costume I look nothing at all like Elvis. It was a big mountain to climb, but for whatever reason, I was determined to climb it." These days, St. Angel cites Presley as one of his favorite singers, along with Bobby Darin, Engelbert Humperdinck and Peter Cetera.

His first show took place at the end of 2005 when he performed at a senior activities center on the northwest side of Chicago: "I had pitched [the idea] to the venue's manager by offering them one hour of free entertainment. My brother and two cousins helped with the sound equipment and music. Surprisingly, I wasn't as nervous as I thought I would be or thought that I should be. I was cloaked in a disguise and not performing as myself, so it was easy to hide behind that. Plus, I had practiced and felt prepared. Since then, I've performed at that venue a couple of times every year. It's always a special experience since that is where it all began for me." A few months after the senior citizen gig, he was hired to play at an Italian restaurant in Rosemont, Illinois. St. Angel recalled, "It was a full house, and everyone close to me, family and friends, attended. I was humbly grateful for their support."

St. Angel's tribute primarily concentrates on the '70s jumpsuit era: "I like the songs, the performances and the production of Elvis in concert starting in 1969 through the '70s the most." Some of his favorites to sing are "Suspicious Minds," "An American Trilogy," and "My Way." St. Angel added, "I include 'Little Darlin' regularly in my sets because I personally enjoy it, and it's a good, quirky tune that people know." Naturally, he sings the hits but will also toss in uncommon songs like "There's a Honky Tonk Angel (Who'll Take Me Back In)" and "The Twelfth of Never." Usually, St. Angel sings along with backing tracks, something he calls "enhanced karaoke": "I use an iPod to carry my songs, and I've had a few experiences where it has locked up on me mid-song. The song simply stops. Something like that can easily rattle your cage, but the key is to never stop performing and no matter what happens—go with the flow because things don't always go as planned."

Regarding jumpsuits, the Aloha Eagle that Presley wore in the 1973 television special *Aloha from Hawaii Via Satellite* is one of St. Angel's favorites: "It is probably the most recognizable by fans and non-fans alike, and it epitomizes the grandiose nature of his persona on stage while capturing the patriotic enthusiasm that Elvis had for his country. I had one but sold it a couple of years ago. I currently have another one in the works, although it's being made with silver stud work vs. the original gold. No matter how well you take care of your suits, gold always tarnishes."

St. Angel, known as the Windy City Elvis, performs 50 shows a year: "I have a full-time job because I have always preferred the stability of a career outside of Elvis. I never flirted with the idea of being a full-time entertainer because even at the most professional level, it's a grind. It's not an easy life in a lot of cases. I like the flexibility of what I created, and at 50, 60 shows a year, I get my fill of performing." Besides paying homage to Presley at public venues, he'll also participate in private events, such as a birthday party, wedding or corporate function. St. Angel commented, "The usual performance time is an hour, but I've done a five-minute guest spot to multiple set shows with costume changes that last a few hours. Afterward, I stick around to say hello to fans and pose for a few photos. It's my way of thanking them for attending the show. I've signed many autographs over the years: on my CDs, my business cards, napkins, Elvis scarves and random body parts.

"I get great satisfaction after a successful performance, and a high of sorts does set in afterward. Very seldom do I go immediately to bed following a show. After taking off the costume and the makeup, I usually have quite an appetite since I don't eat very heavily before the show, so I'll indulge in a big meal in front of the TV. I look forward to that ritual of winding down."

Gib Maynard

In 2018, Gib Maynard placed in the Top Ten at the Nashville Elvis Festival. The following year, he made the Top Five: "I am very proud of that progress and look forward to continuing to compete in that awesome festival. I have made the finals in numerous other festivals as well."

Seven. "Walk a Mile in My Shoes"

Maynard plans to enter the Ultimate in Memphis. "I am always proud of the winner of the competition because I know how much hard work it takes to get there. It truly is a brotherhood."[7] In only a few short years, he has grown in popularity among his peers and fans alike.

Maynard was born on November 25, 1990, in Tyler, Texas. He became an avid Presley fan at age six. Two years later, he performed his first tribute in his parents' living room, lip-synching for about 15 of his relatives: "They had a blast, and I did too. I wore a white jumpsuit with small hand-sewn sequins that my grandmother made me. I believe that my mother still has it." He began singing in a Baptist church at age ten: "My first song was 'Amazing Grace,' which ironically is now my favorite Elvis gospel song." Early on, he also took an interest in playing the piano. While Presley is his primary musical influence, Maynard adds, "Being raised in the church, my first musical influences were definitely Southern gospel artists. I love lots of genres, though, especially blues and gospel."

The stage show *A Tribute to the Million Dollar Quartet* provided Gib Maynard with the opportunity to play the same high school auditorium stage in Gladewater, Texas, that Elvis Presley had played in 1955 (courtesy Gib Maynard).

You Sound Just Like...

Thanks to his theater major at Tyler Junior College in Tyler, Texas, Maynard has a background in acting: "I learned a lot about costume design, stage makeup and hair. Also, acting exercises that help get you into character." For a year, he was part of the cast in *A Tribute to the Million Dollar Quartet*, which took place in Gladewater, Texas. He performed at the Gladewater High School gymnasium, on the same stage where Presley performed in 1955: "I can't even explain the emotions and the energy that surged through my body being there at the same location. It was for sure a surreal moment for me." On February 28, 2018, Maynard made a triumphant return to the stage show for a performance at the Gladewater Opry.

In August 2017, Maynard decided to professionally become an Elvis Tribute Artist: "It took a lot of preparation. Initially, I lost about 80 pounds and got myself into shape physically as well as vocally. My very first Elvis gig was at a restaurant here in my hometown. Everyone had an amazing time and was blown away. As I look back on that, I [realize that I] have grown so much in my craft since then." He admitted that he is constantly working at perfecting his homage, practicing at least 10 to 15 hours a week: "I have definitely worn my voice out. The best remedy to keep my voice healthy is warm herbal tea, and I like to add fresh lemon and honey to it. I also like the honey and lemon throat lozenges."

Theaters, restaurants and bars around the country are his typical gigs: "I normally perform for two hours. It takes about 15 minutes to style the hair and about an hour to do the makeup. I like to use argon oil on my hair. My favorite jumpsuit is the King of Spades, and I just recently acquired a replica of it. When selecting songs, I always try to consider the audience, the occasion and the location. I usually include Elvis' biggest hits, such as 'Suspicious Minds,' 'Love Me,' 'C.C. Rider' and 'That's All Right.' I love to sing 'Suspicious Minds' because it has fantastic lyrics, music and movements to it. I would have to say, though, that my favorites are all of Elvis' country songs."

Sometimes Maynard will get a request for a song with which he isn't that familiar: "If I know the song well enough, and I'm in a casual setting like a restaurant, I will pull the song up on YouTube and try to sing it for the guest. It's all about making Elvis fans happy.

"It is definitely hard to come down after a performance. I try to relax by soaking in a hot bath, sipping a glass of wine, and reflecting back on the show." Similar to other performers, he has had his share of pratfalls: "The most frequent thing that happens to me is, I get so caught up in a song or watching the audience that I forget the lyrics, which is embarrassing. But Elvis did it too."

Bill Cherry

Bill Cherry became aware of Elvis Tribute Artists when his parents took him to see Ron Furr in Collinsville, Illinois, in 1978. Cherry recalled, "I'll never forget all the people who were there, the excitement in the room as the music started, and the drums beating to the intro of 'C.C. Rider.' Ron appeared from the back of the room [surrounded by] four bodyguards dressed in black, wearing black sunglasses. Ron was in the middle, wearing a white jumpsuit. The crowd went wild, standing on their chairs just to get a look at him as he walked to the stage. I was blown away. At that moment, he was Elvis, and everyone went back in time with him. It was right then that I knew I could and had to do this. It was my calling; I felt it in my very soul."[8] Eight years later, Cherry made his dream a reality by stepping onto the stage as Presley. And in 2009, he was crowned the winner in the Ultimate Elvis Presley Tribute Artist Contest in Memphis.

At five years old, Cherry started singing, and it was an old gospel hymn. "My father was a minister of a small church, where he sang and played guitar quite often. While at home in the afternoon or evening, he would take out his guitar and play old country or gospel music, and sometimes I would sing [along] with him." During Cherry's formative years, he was exposed to Elvis Presley: "I recall we had about four or five Elvis albums, and when one of his movies came on television, my mother would always let me know, and we would watch it together. I loved his voice—the way he sang, the way he looked, his sense of humor, the race cars and the speedboats [featured in the movies], and no matter the obstacles, he always won the race. To me, he was the coolest and still is today."

Cherry's mother never got to see him perform in front of an audience as she passed away in 2000: "However, she had a front row [seat] to every performance I did for her in our living room. When I was 11 years old, I would put an Elvis record on the record player, turn out the lights, and my father would hold a flashlight, which would be my spotlight, and I would perform [along with] the record. It was so exciting for me to do these little shows for my parents. They loved it and encouraged me to continue." Cherry's biggest influences are Presley and The Beatles. He's also a fan of classic rock and classic country.

You Sound Just Like...

In 1986, Cherry entered the Elvis tribute world during a competition held at a small Memphis club called Bad Bob Vapors. "I felt the audience reaction was very good, more than I had anticipated, which made me want to do more." Several other competitions followed: "I continued unsuccessfully with those until 1995. At that point, I had a family, which included a son, so I decided it was time to re-think my situation. In 2006, I was working as a welder in a steel foundry when a friend told me about an Elvis competition that was being held by Elvis Presley Enterprises. That got my attention.

"I wasn't sure of myself; after all, it had been 12 years since I had been on stage. However, with the encouragement of family and friends, I started singing along with Elvis again— getting my voice back into shape. I also had a beard at the time, and I was hesitant

Bill Cherry won the Tupelo preliminary and the Ultimate Elvis Competition in Memphis back-to-back. His prize for the latter: $20,000, a gold championship belt and a year contract with *Legends in Concert* (courtesy Bill Cherry).

but knew I had to shave it off. I kept the sideburns. When I put on the Elvis glasses and looked in the mirror, it was like stepping back in time. I transform into Elvis when I put on the jumpsuit and walk out on stage; the character takes over. I am [still] shy to a certain extent but mostly private. I just hide behind the makeup and costume. It's like Halloween; you're safe behind the mask."

Seven. "Walk a Mile in My Shoes"

Cherry won the Ultimate Elvis Tribute Artist Contest in Memphis. In doing so, he was the first to ever win the Tupelo preliminary and the Ultimate Elvis consecutively. Winning a preliminary with 20 to 25 competitors is a prerequisite to qualify for the Ultimate. Cherry acknowledged, "I have won many awards throughout the years, including the Heart of the King award, but I'm most proud of winning the Ultimate Elvis Tribute Artist Contest. I received $20,000, a gold championship belt and a year contract with *Legends in Concert*. ...Throughout the years, I have performed at most of their venues, including Branson, Atlantic City and Las Vegas." *Time* magazine called him one of the Top Elvis Tribute Artists in the World: "I was very honored by this." Since then, Cherry has performed regularly in theaters. His largest audience included 10,000 spectators.

Cherry tries to choose songs that he feels the fans want to hear, but he also likes to throw in an occasional wild card, one that's not so popular yet fun to do, such as "I've Got a Thing About You Baby." Cherry admitted that he has many favorites in Presley's catalogue: "On stage, I would have to say 'Suspicious Minds' because it is a fan favorite and fun to perform, and 'My Way' because I feel it is very fitting to Elvis' life and career." He will also take audience suggestions but added, "Sometimes if I get a request for a song that I'm not totally familiar with, I will try and do just a few lines as a teaser."

There have been some embarrassing moments: "As with any live show, things can go wrong, such as walking out on stage as the audience is cheering and anticipating the first note to come out of your mouth, but as you reach for the microphone you discover the microphone is off, or putting on your guitar and having it fall to the floor because the strap broke, or losing power in the middle of the show. And let's not forget to mention tripping and falling as you walk out on stage. They are ice-breakers for sure. I have learned to just laugh it off, along with the audience."

As far as wardrobe choices go, Cherry prefers the jumpsuits that Presley wore later in his career: "They are beautifully embroidered designs. I have owned many replicas of these suits, such as the Phoenix, the Indian, the Bicentennial, the Alpine, the Gypsy, the American Eagle and my favorite, the iconic Sundial, which Elvis wore on his final tour and during the TV special for CBS."

In 2018, Cherry decided to share another of his passions with the public when he opened a record store called Monster Vinyl, in his hometown of Collinsville, Illinois: "I wanted a business that consisted of vintage records, toys, movie posters and monsters. These are things I have always had an interest in and thought I would share with others."

Ted Torres Martin

Ted Torres Martin has a background in theater, playing in works such as *One Flew Over the Cuckoo's Nest* and *Death of a Salesman*, and this has aided him in his portrayal of Elvis Presley: "I have a different approach when it comes to my act, and I believe it really has helped. When I am on stage, I do feel like I get into acting mode to portray and channel Elvis as best as I can. Like Elvis, I have always been extremely shy. I still am to a certain extent. As for stage fright, I always get nervous before a show. I get over it by flipping that internal switch and getting into acting mode. After the first song, I am just fine. When I am off-stage, I am always myself."[9] His early stage experiences have also been beneficial in helping him create his own musicals.

At a very young age, Martin began singing. He stated, "I was always around music since my parents were both performers and in the entertainment business." Martin started learning chords on the guitar at age ten: "My father taught me how to play. He was an amazing guitar player and recording artist. I get by, but I wish I could play like he did. I can also play a couple of other instruments, including the viola, which I studied for seven years. Not many people know that I studied classical music and music theory."

At 11, he became an Elvis Presley fan: "I first saw him on TV when they showed the movie *Jailhouse Rock*. [There was] something about him that I really connected with. Plus, I knew I wanted to comb my hair like him. I just thought he had really cool hair, and it stuck with me."

One of Martin's first gigs was singing at an Elvis convention in Orlando, Florida: "I've always been extremely shy, but when I got on stage and started performing as Elvis in the 1950s, it's like something took over me. D.J. Fontana was behind me on the drums. That was nerve-wracking, but he really encouraged me to keep going. We remained friends for many years. He was a great man. The people loved it, and it made me feel great because I loved singing Elvis' songs." Martin cited Presley and his parents as his main musical influences, but he also loves Bobby Darin, Dean Martin, Sammy Davis Jr., Solomon Burke, Frank Sinatra, Roy Orbison, Chris Isaak and Merle Haggard, just to

Seven. "Walk a Mile in My Shoes"

name a few. He noted, "I have a very eclectic taste in music, so I have been influenced by many amazing singers."

Theaters are his main venues: "I've been lucky to play some amazingly beautiful theaters all over the world. I believe my largest audience was around 8,000 people, many years ago in Daytona Beach, Florida. That was quite the thrill." Every era of Presley's career has been covered by Martin, but his primary focus is 1968 to 1971 because he believes he resembles Presley the most during that time. "My favorite [material] to perform would be from 1969 and 1970 because I just love how much energy Elvis had during that period in his career. He was really going for it, and it was very exciting for him. However, I plan my shows according to what I am requested to do. I usually stick to songs that I really enjoy and that I know the people want to hear. A lot of times, I put in a few obscure ones that I love and that I want to share with the public." Some of his favorites to sing are "What Now My Love," "Hurt," "Suspicious Minds" and "There's Always Me." He added, "Luckily, I pretty much know just about every song Elvis ever recorded. Once in a while, you get someone who will yell out something like 'There's No Room to Rumba in a Sports Car,' a song from the movie *Fun in Acapulco*. That has a tendency

One of Ted Torres Martin's first gigs as Elvis Presley was at an Orlando, Florida, convention. Martin has always been extremely shy, but when he got on stage and performed as Presley, he forgot about everything and embraced the role (courtesy Ted Torres Martin).

to throw me off, but I sing a line just to please them and then go on with my show. People are usually fine with that." As for dressing the part, the Caped Fringe jumpsuit is his favorite, and he owns a replica.

Martin was asked to participate in the celebration of the 50th Anniversary of Elvis' debut at the Hilton in Las Vegas: "I had been lucky to grace that stage before, but that time around was extremely special because it was my own hour-and-a-half show on the same stage. I used the same dressing room that Elvis used and the same elevator, which added to the magic. I was very honored to have been chosen. We did two nights there, and they were both sold out. It was like a spiritual experience for me, absolutely incredible." Then there was the time he played at the Peabody Hotel in Memphis with The Jordanaires: "I happened to walk to the front of the stage, and I hadn't noticed where it ended, so I fell right off the stage. Ray Walker, in his very deep voice, then asked me if I was okay. It was a moment I won't ever forget, and I don't think anyone else has either." While he loves doing tributes, relaxing after a show can be challenging: "I am usually pretty wired for hours after my show. I manage to relax the best that I can by spending time with my family and friends, getting something to eat, and talking. Sometimes I'll grab my guitar and play more music in my room for an hour or two."

Even though Martin is best known for his Presley tribute, he has also paid homage to another favorite, The Everly Brothers: "You can't top those beautiful harmonies. They were so talented. I really love their songs 'Till I Kissed You' and 'Crying in the Rain.' I have played Phil Everly a few times, the most with my good buddy Lance Lipinsky. It's always a great time. I have also enjoyed performing that act with Dean Z." Rick Nelson is another artist whom Martin has showcased onstage: "I am a huge fan of Rick's music, but I don't try to impersonate him. Other than all of the 1950s material, Rick had a lot of great songs in the late '60s and '70s. He was very instrumental in bringing that California country-rock sound to the mainstream. A lot of people don't give him credit for that. Some of my favorite songs are 'Lonesome Town,' 'California' and 'Five Minutes More.'"

The tribute artists industry is highly lucrative, but many of its stars aspire to branch out, and Martin is no exception: "When I started writing music, it was considered Americana. After almost getting signed to a major record label at 27, they tried to convince me to choose what I wanted to do because they couldn't categorize it. The record deal didn't materialize; the company wanted ownership of my songs, and I didn't want to do that. I then switched to writing country music, which I love. I wrote a song called 'Your Kiss,' which I submitted for a duet album. I was told that Garth Brooks and Trisha Yearwood were going to record it. I had heard that they really liked it. However, the album did not happen. That's just the way the music industry works. I am still actively writing, and I am in the process of trying to put a new project together."

Besides trying to create a solo career based on his original material, Martin also writes and produces musicals: "I love making my own stage shows, like *Back to Live*. The idea for that came to me in a dream. I realized that not many people covered an amazing part of Elvis' career, which was 1969. It took me about a month to write, but it took almost a year for it to materialize on the stage. I premiered the show in Deland, Florida, a few years back. [On the show,] I was lucky enough to have such talented ladies and good friends, The Sweet Inspirations, plus an amazing lineup of musicians, including strings and horns. We got great reviews. I was able to take the show out of state a few times. We did sold-out shows across the U.S., including performances in Memphis. The finale took place in Los Angeles. I knew that we had something special. *On Stage* is a production that I wrote not long ago, although it's pretty much part two of *Back to Live*. It's different in that there is not a lot of acting; it's more a straightforward concert. I've gone above and beyond to try and make this as authentic as possible with details, even down to the microphones. The whole idea of the show is to make people feel like they are back in 1970, experiencing Elvis in concert in Las Vegas. We have only performed the show a few times, but got amazing reviews from the *Las Vegas Review-Journal*. We intend on bringing *On Stage* to audiences across the U.S. and hopefully Europe and other parts of the world. That's my goal. I like to bring the Elvis fans something different, and I hope they appreciate it."

In 2014, director William Bryan contacted Martin about providing the vocals for his short *Nobody*, based on Presley's talent show appearance in his final year of high school: "William has always had tremendous respect for my vocal abilities. When he approached me with the idea of including the song 'Till I Waltz Again with You,' I was a little nervous. There's not an existing recording of Elvis singing that song, but I decided to take on the task. For about a month straight, I tried to absorb [all the music] that he listened to at the time—country, pop, rhythm and blues, blues, opera, you name it. Then I sat down and listened to Teresa Brewer's version of the song. After that, I listened to all of the existing Elvis demos that were recorded at Memphis Recording Service. That's how I came up with the way that I thought he had sung his version. Shortly after, I flew to Memphis and recorded at Sun Studio. Once the director and people affiliated with the film listened to my version, they all agreed that is how it would have sounded if there was an actual recording by Elvis. I was very honored and flattered by all the positive comments and accolades given to me. It was a great project to be a part of, and everybody did an amazing job. I will always hold the movie dear to my heart."

That same year, Martin won the Heart of the King award. "That was a very special moment for me, and it came when I was going through a very difficult chapter in my life. I had just recently lost my father, so being there to accept the award was extremely emotional for me. I knew that I was flying to Las Vegas to receive it, so I had a speech prepared. I also performed. Only a select few in this industry have been given the honor. It is one of the awards that I am most proud of because I worked so hard for it—blood, sweat and tears. It made me feel like hard work really does pay off. The award is in our display case here at my home.

"My favorite aspect of paying tribute to Elvis is singing his songs to the real Elvis fans out there. Also, it's very special when I get to travel around the world, bringing his music to audiences in places he was never able to go. The whole experience is always extremely magical to me. I just love and respect his music, and him as a person. I am very lucky to be able to do what I love for a living."

Johnny Thompson

Johnny Thompson has quite a résumé—model, actor, Elvis Tribute Artist, opening act for Eddie Money, The Goo Goo Dolls, The Platters and The Beach Boys. He explained how he got the opportunity to work with the latter: "I was hired by a group out of Rochester, New York, for a party they put on every year for their employees. I didn't know who the other act was until I arrived. I shared a green room with The Beach Boys [including Mike Love and Bruce Johnston], so we got to meet and hang out. I did my show, then I wanted to see them perform, so I changed and sat in the back of the audience. There were about 3000 people [in attendance]. After the show, I went back to the green room and Bruce said, 'Johnny, we were looking for you backstage. We wanted to do a couple of Elvis songs with you.' They said I reminded them of John Stamos. I

Seven. "Walk a Mile in My Shoes"

told them I had been out in the audience watching the show. There was a missed opportunity."[10]

In 2011, Thompson moved to Asia. Two years later, he started touring with The Platters. Cruise ships, casinos and theaters keep him active on the tribute artists' scene, but he also finds time to be a minister and song leader in his church. Thompson preaches about once a month.

Growing up, Thompson lived the life of a Navy brat. He was born in Fort Worth, Texas, and lived in Texas until he was eight years old, then moved to California, Georgia, Mississippi and Maryland (every two years, the family relocated). He attended 14 different schools. At ten, he began singing in the church: "I attend the Church of Christ, so we sing everything *a cappella*." Around the same time, he gave his first performance as Elvis Presley: "For the neighborhood kids, I lip-synched to 'Jailhouse Rock' on a stage my brother and I built in our backyard." The kids donated money, so he purchased the album *Elvis Gold*.

Presley was an integral part of Thompson's upbringing: "My father was a huge Elvis fan. In the 1970s, he had taken me to see my first three Elvis impersonators. Thanks to

Johnny Thompson was featured in the music videos of both Katy Perry's "Waking Up in Vegas" and Carrie Underwood's "Last Name." He beat out hundreds of Elvis Tribute Artists who had auditioned (photograph by Justice Howard; courtesy Johnny Thompson).

You Sound Just Like...

listening to Elvis in my dad's '69 Camaro, watching his movies together, and playing his records, we always had this Elvis bond. In 1976, my dad saw Elvis at the Tarrant County Convention Center in Fort Worth. We were vacationing in Biloxi, Mississippi, a year later when we learned that Elvis had died. We all were really upset. It was like losing a family member." Thompson's parents were divorced, so he divided his time between his mom and dad's.

His mother was also a music fan. Her vast collection of oldies albums were constantly played by Thompson: The Platters, Dean Martin, Herb Alpert, Tom Jones, Engelbert Humperdinck, Neil Diamond, and The Beatles. Thompson cites Presley, George Jones, George Strait, Dwight Yoakam, Carrie Underwood, Cheap Trick, The Eagles, Styx and INXS in his list of favorite singers.

After high school graduation, Thompson moved back to Texas to live with his father and attend college in Kilgore. He took up playing the guitar and joined the college jazz band. Eventually, he became manager of the Kilgore College Rangerettes, a troupe of 65 dancers who performed annually at the Cotton Bowl and appear in the Macy's Thanksgiving Day Parade. In the late '80s, Thompson moved to Chicago to pursue acting: "I studied theater at the College of DuPage. I had the exact same teachers as John and Jim Belushi. I also took private acting lessons in Chicago."

A girl in Thompson's acting class suggested that he model. He gave it a shot, and for eight years, he was successful. To take pictures of him, he hired photographer Kevin Currin, "who was recommended by my agent at Chicago Model Group. He answered the door and said he was in the middle of another shoot, with Halle Berry. I had shown up in a black leather jacket and black jeans, and she was wearing the exact same outfit, so I said to her, 'We have got to do some shots together. It's fate.' She agreed, and we did some amazing, fun and sexy shots. We both used them on our model company cards. Over the next year, I ran into Halle at all my catalogue shoots in Chicago, Michigan and Wisconsin. We became friends. She then moved to L.A. to do a TV show, *Living Dolls*. While I was doing a modeling gig for Bloomingdale's in Chicago, [she was in town] and saw me. She came up, hugged me and told me all about her new career in L.A. and the TV show. Halle said she knew no one there, lived alone in a big house and asked me to move to L.A. I told her I would have to think about that. In Chicago, she was with her boyfriend, whom she said was jealous, so she couldn't give me her new number in front of him. She told me to call our agent, and they would give me her number. I waited a week or so to call, but when I did, the agency had gone bankrupt, and the phones were shut off. Years later, I tried reaching out through her fan club website, but nothing ever worked out."

After calling it quits as a model, Thompson decided to take a job as a singing telegram: "I had already done comedy singing telegrams as Rent-a-Nerd. One day I heard the agent say that they wished they had an Elvis as they had gotten a lot of calls for one. I said, 'I can sing like Elvis,' but I was blond and looked nothing like him except for my hairstyle. However, I told them I would put together an act, come back and audition for them. I learned five songs, including 'Can't Help Falling in Love,' and went back two weeks later with a '50s jacket and black mousse in my hair. I auditioned for all the ladies at the agency. The owner started crying when I did 'Can't Help Falling in Love.' I said, 'Is something wrong?' She said, 'You sound just like Elvis. You are hired!' I did that for the next three years. My first paid gig as Elvis was as a singing telegram for the Chicago city alderman and his family. They hired me to sing five songs at a birthday party." There were about a hundred people in attendance, and the ladies went berserk as if they were seeing the King himself. More private party gigs followed, throughout Chicago, Indiana and Wisconsin. "I first approached [portraying] Elvis as an actor, learning to break him down as a person and then as a character, mimicking his movements and speech. It wasn't just his signature moves while singing but also the way he walked across the stage, placed his hands on his hips, pointed to people onstage, and shook his head. A lot goes into the portrayal." Thompson spent hundreds of hours watching and studying video clips of Presley. Eventually, he entered contests and worked with the Elvis Conventions in Chicago. From 1997 to 2000, he ran the Elvis Entertainers Network along with Nance Fox.

Next, he founded the Professional Elvis Impersonators Association. In June 2002, they had a convention at the Lady Luck Casino in Las Vegas. Twenty impersonators from around the world participated, and Glen Glenn and Kay Wheeler, friends of Presley's, were special guests. Thompson had moved to Las Vegas in September 2001 and was employed at the Elvis-a-Rama Museum: "I auditioned and worked for them for about nine months. I did 33 shows, six days a week; some were ten minutes while others were 30 and 60 minutes. After 9/11, for a year, Las Vegas was a ghost town, so I was lucky to have found work."

In 2005, MTV recruited Thompson: "The producers contacted my manager at the time, Kristy Royle of Royal Talent, and said they were auditioning Elvises in Las Vegas. They wanted an ETA to host the red carpet for *Total Request Live*. Some of the show's producers came and watched my show at the Plaza Hotel Casino. They called Kristy and said they had found their guy. I did two days of filming for them [as Elvis]." Elvis Presley Enterprises granted MTV permission to call him Elvis. "Also on that show were The Black Eyed Peas and The Pussycat Dolls with host Vanessa Lachey. Hosting the red carpet for the *MTV Movie Awards* was both nerve-wracking and exciting. The first person I interviewed was Lacey Chabert. I also spoke with Jessica Alba, Jessica Simpson, Eva Mendes, Ryan Gosling, Jessica Biel, Quentin Tarantino and Jon Heder. When I talked to Hilary Swank, I asked her why she hadn't won the previous year's 'Best Kiss Award,' and she said, 'I don't know. Come on.' She then [proceeded to] make out with me for the camera. That was one of the best days in my career."

Thompson received additional worldwide attention when he appeared in music videos for both Katy Perry and Carrie Underwood: "I had an agent in Las Vegas who set up the auditions. In Carrie's video for 'Last Name,' I played the minister who marries her and her beau. For Katy's 'Waking Up in Vegas,' multiple ETAs, including myself, danced in a scene with her. Both were a lot of fun. I actually spent several hours talking with Carrie."

Throughout his career as an ETA, Thompson has performed at numerous venues worldwide—theaters, casinos, NBA games, NFL games and restaurants: "The largest audience was 100,000 people at a New York Jets game, where I did the halftime show." One of his scariest experiences occurred in Lansing, Michigan, in front of 5000 people: "At one point, a large group of women rushed the stage, pulled me off and tore at my jumpsuit. My manager at the time, Nance Fox, was standing backstage and yelled at security to help me. It took ten security officers to get me away from those women and back onstage."

Thompson's shows run between 75 and 90 minutes. Al Dvorin, famous for announcing "Elvis has left the building," befriended Thompson after they met at the Elvis Fantasy Fest in Portage, Indiana, in 1998: "I did many shows with Al. Once, he and I were backstage at the House of Blues in Chicago, and he told me that Elvis never sang over 90 minutes. Al said, 'Always leave them wanting more, then they will come back and see you again.'" Thompson used to choose songs that he loved to perform, but then he realized that he needed to sing the popular hits everyone wants to hear, such as "Can't Help Falling in Love," "In the Ghetto," "Suspicious Minds," "An American Trilogy,"

"Always on My Mind" and "My Way." He acknowledged, "Elvis did 750 songs, and I do roughly 125 of them. I have so many [personal] favorites, but if I had to narrow it down to one; 'Can't Help Falling in Love' would be it. That was the song I first recorded at a mall studio in 1987. When I did the tape, the engineer came out of the booth and said, 'Man, you gotta hear this!' He played it back, and I said, 'Who is that?' He said, 'That is your voice. Man, you sound just like Elvis.' That song started my career."

Martial arts are a Thompson specialty (he has taught Filipino police and military in hand-to-hand combat), and he has incorporated a lot of karate moves into his stage act: "I have 35 years of training experience. Bruce Lee was my hero. I hold four black belts and certifications in six martial arts. Having the knowledge that Elvis had, and being able to break down his moves, I have an advantage over others who have no idea what he is doing with kicks and punches. Being able to replicate those moves with authenticity makes a world of difference.

"I just try to capture Elvis as best as I can on stage. I want people to walk out and go, 'Wow, that's what it was like to see Elvis. That's what it was like to experience one of his concerts.'"[11]

Dwight Icenhower

In 2007, Elvis Presley Enterprises held their first-ever Elvis Tribute Artist contest in Memphis, Tennessee. Twenty-four individuals vied for the Ultimate Elvis crown. Shawn Klush won. Nine years later, Dwight Icenhower took home the title. Besides $20,000 and the 60-CD box set *Elvis Presley—the Album Collection*, the other prize that came with winning was a contract with *Legends in Concert*. However, Icenhower was already working with the production.

He stated, "I performed at the Branson, Myrtle Beach and Las Vegas venues. I enjoyed my time there, but after a while, it became too routine. I went out on stage and sang the same six songs every single night. I was grateful for the opportunity, but I was happy to move on to other things."[12]

Icenhower continues to pay tribute to Presley but also has aspirations of performing his homage to Elton John on a more regular basis. He acknowledged, "It used to take me a long time to get ready as both, but now I have it down to a science, and it takes me less than 45 minutes."

You Sound Just Like…

In 2016, Dwight Icenhower won the Ultimate Elvis Competition in Memphis. A few of the songs he performed for the judges were "Suspicious Minds," "Unchained Melody" and "You Gave Me a Mountain." Icenhower remembered, "I had no clue prior to winning that I was going to. I just knew that I [had] given it all I had and was hoping for the best. It was a dream come true to win the crown" (courtesy Dwight Icenhower).

Icenhower was born on May 21, 1981, in Southeast Ohio. At five years of age, his mother introduced him to the music of Elvis Presley: "I always watched Elvis' movies." In his sophomore year of high school, he began singing: "I sang my first song, 'All Shook Up,' at a variety show called *American Pop Forever*." Icenhower then gained quite a bit of experience thanks to the fair he attended in Meigs County, Ohio: "Every year they would have karaoke on the main bandstand, and I would always chicken out until one time I finally got up and sang." His musical influences are Presley, Elton John, Billy Joel, The Beatles, Roy Orbison, Ricky Nelson and The Rolling Stones.

In the mid–1990s, while Icenhower was still in high school, he became a fan of Elton John: "One year, for a show, our high school marching band played the music of Elton, so that got me curious about the rest of his catalogue. As I began to learn more and more about his music, I also became interested in singing his songs. It started as a fluke at karaoke, then I built up the nerve to give it a shot on stage, so I went out and bought myself a funny-looking costume and some big glasses. My first show as Elton was in Omaha, Nebraska. I perform as Elton maybe eight to ten times a year, but I'm looking to do it much more in the future. Elton has never seen my tribute, but I have seen him over 90 times in concert. I sat in the front row at one of them, and I shook his hand. That was as close as I got to meeting him."

Theaters, cruise ships and festivals are Icenhower's main venues: "I do a lot more traveling these days instead of playing in stationary venues. However, I play a great dinner theater, Visani, in Port Charlotte, Florida. Sometimes my band and I will play there two or three times a month. We always have a blast there."

Regarding the setlists for his Presley shows: "I always have to include the classics and the hits, but I also like to stretch out and do some of the B sides in my shows. I think it keeps it fresh for me and the audience. Sometimes I will get requests, and usually I will give it a go even if I don't know the song." One of his favorites to perform live is "Are You Lonesome Tonight?": "I just love the way Elvis' voice sounds in that song, and I try to recreate it." Another song he really enjoys is "Three Corn Patches": "Some people laugh at me because it's such a rare song, but I love the funny lyrics and the bluesy beat of it. I only sing it on occasion, though."

Throughout the years, Icenhower has racked up 75 first-place awards in Elvis tribute contests worldwide. However, the one that gained him the most notoriety was the Ultimate Elvis Contest, which he won in 2016: "I can't remember all of the songs that I sang but a few of them were 'Suspicious Minds,' 'Unchained Melody' and 'You Gave Me a Mountain.' I felt so good about the performance, and the crowd response was great. I knew that I had given it all I had and was hoping for the best, but my mind was blown [when I won]. It was a dream come true." In 2018, Icenhower was chosen by Apple to be the lead Elvis Tribute Artist in their FaceTime campaign: "I was sought out by a talent scout who was sent to Chicago to attend a festival I was headlining. It was so exciting to see the commercial during the Super Bowl. Being part of that worldwide campaign for Apple was an honor and a great learning experience."

You Sound Just Like...

John Lyons

Most Elvis Tribute Artists devote their careers to paying homage to Presley. John Lyons is an exception since he has a regular full-time job. His tribute is something he usually only does on weekends.

A lifelong Presley fan, Lyons began singing along to Presley albums at a young age. He later had a band named Montage that regularly featured Presley tunes. He was the lead singer until 2003. In 2009, Lyons became an ETA. These days, his act also showcases the talents of his wife Peggy and their son Jonathan.

John Lyons was born on October 31, 1962, in Evergreen Park, Illinois. His dad worked two jobs to put five children through private grammar school, high school and college. Lyons recalled, "We had little money for recreation, but we had a turntable. I loved music and sang along to all of our 45 RPM records. I've been singing so long that I couldn't tell you the first song I sang, but I know my mom sure liked when I sang 'Georgy Girl' by The Seekers. I sang a lot—to The Monkees, The Beatles, anything in the Top 40, and of course Elvis. My sister and I conjured

John Lyons has had a few mishaps during his tenure as Elvis Presley. A few years ago, he was doing a private show with his son Jonathan, who portrays the 1950s version of Presley, when his voice went out on the first song. He explained, "I had been sick but thought I had recovered enough to do this show. I guess not. Jonathan stepped in and completed the whole show by himself. I don't think I have ever canceled a show, but that one came close" (courtesy John Lyons).

up an imaginary band, and we often performed in the basement together, each taking turns as the lead singer and then as the backup singer.

"Mary is a huge Elvis fan. Throughout our youth, she purchased every Elvis album she could get her hands on. We played those albums so much that I'm surprised we didn't wear them out. Those songs became a big part of what we sang in that mock band of ours. Soon, I had the stylings and intonations of Elvis down [pat]. It just felt natural. I wasn't trying to imitate him. I just wanted the song to sound like the record. Over time, I became a very good imitator of many vocalists, not an impressionist like Rich Little, but rather an imitator of their style of singing."[13] Lyons' musical influences are REO Speedwagon, Queen, Dire Straits, The Beatles, Chuck Berry, Little Richard, The Monkees, Herman's Hermits, Jerry Lee Lewis and Presley. He admitted, "I'm a rock and roller at heart."

In the eighth grade, Lyons and some classmates started a band called Montage: "As we grew in popularity, we moved from modern-day rock and roll to classics and wedding music because the gigs our agent booked for us were corporate parties and weddings. My sister became a backup vocalist, and she made sure we had Elvis songs in our sets. My bandmates got a kick out of me doing his songs and often asked me to sing 'Jailhouse Rock.' I would always appease them and sing it *a cappella*. The response was always positive, and it really helped my confidence grow.

"Around the same time, my sister gave me my first T-shirt with John 'Elvis' Lyons on the back. I wore it proudly, and when people asked why the name was on the shirt, I'd tell them, and then if they wanted, I would give them a taste. I continued to gain an appreciation for Elvis' music and his performances. I emulated him more and more each time our band played. Elvis eventually became a daily part of my life and a part of every show. I had the opportunity to perform in a talent show on a Carnival cruise ship. I could choose any song I wanted, and I chose 'Jailhouse Rock.' This was for a big crowd, and they loved it. For me, the absolute capper was seeing him live in concert, twice—in October 1976 and May 1977 at the Chicago Stadium. My sister and I went, and he blew us away. The place was electric. When Elvis hit the stage and started singing, the place exploded. It was as if something magical happened when he walked out onto that stage. My heart jumped; I cheered, and I was mesmerized. When he performed 'Hurt,' he brought the house down. His voice was crisp, clear and more powerful in person than I ever thought it could be. It was an experience I will never forget. After seeing him in concert, I was stoked. I couldn't wait to get out and perform again. I knew there was no way to replicate what he was doing, but he gave me the energy and desire to perform. He made me a better entertainer."

At the time, Lyons had no desire to become an Elvis Tribute Artist; it wasn't until after his band broke up, he got married, and his two children became teenagers that he was presented with the opportunity: "My sister was getting married for the second time and really didn't have the money for a band or a DJ, so she asked me. My family is known for doing some kind of surprise—songs, skits, roasts, etc.—so I got the bright idea, since my sister is a huge Elvis fan, that I would rent a jumpsuit and Elvis would make an appearance. I performed most of my DJ duties in proper wedding attire, but I had my wife Peggy take over several songs in, so I could slip out and change into the Elvis jumpsuit. Then, on musical cue, I appeared and surprised my sister by singing a set of her favorites. The performance was a hit. My own mother didn't recognize me.

"After a couple more family parties, I was hired by a guest to perform at her birthday party at a sports bar in Milwaukee. The actual party consisted of about 15 people, so I thought it would be in some small side room. Instead, their table was right in the middle of a packed bar. The place was full because a pub crawl was going on, and a huge crowd had hit the bar just as I was [about] to go on. Everyone loved it. That was my first paying gig, and the adrenaline rush was overwhelming. It was then that I realized I wanted to keep doing it."

Lyons' tribute is not a full-time gig but rather a hobby. He has a regular job working for Haemonetics, a blood management company; he's a manager in the plasma division. "My company doesn't have weekend hours, but I am limited to the number of shows I can do in a year. I average between 60 and 70. There are times when I play Friday through Sunday and other times where I have multiple shows in one day and none the next. If a show comes up during the week that I really want to play, I will take time off from my day job to do it. As for performing for my co-workers, I like keeping the two separate. A few have seen my show and were generally impressed, but they were also shocked by my onstage persona. They know me as pretty low-key and mild-mannered at work. Everyone needs an outlet, and performing is mine. I become a different person when I put the jumpsuit on."

For Lyons, resembling Presley is the most challenging aspect of the tribute: "I don't look like him, but I take pride in getting quality jumpsuits from Pro Elvis and having realistic backing tracks. I purchase my tracks from the EP Project Group. They are a group of musicians who reproduce Elvis' concert songs note for note. Some even feature members of the TCB Band. I love these tracks as they totally capture the sound of a live Elvis concert. Cheap karaoke tracks just don't cut it. I paint a picture and draw the fans in with the jumpsuit, the music and the vocals. I try to capture as much of the ambiance of an Elvis concert as I can, so I don't have to impersonate him down to the last detail." The setlists primarily focus on Presley's career in the 1970s: "The opening is always 'Also Sprach Zarathustra,' the theme from *2001: A Space Odyssey*, then straight into 'C.C. Rider' or 'That's All Right.' Other staples are 'Burning Love,' 'Jailhouse Rock,' 'Teddy Bear/Don't Be Cruel,' 'How Great Thou Art' and 'An American Trilogy.' The closer is 'Can't Help Falling in Love' followed by the traditional outro theme and 'Elvis has left the building.'"

Lyons commented, "He was a religious man, and so am I, so being able to perform 'How Great Thou Art' is an honor. I also enjoy performing 'Hurt' and 'You Gave Me a Mountain.' However, the show-stopper and probably my favorite to sing is 'An American Trilogy.' I love the song's dynamics, and it allows me to explore all the ranges of Elvis' voice. It always ends in a standing ovation." As for duets with his wife, his favorites are "Love Me Tender," "And I Love You So" and "I'm So Lonesome I Could Cry": "Peggy, who has a background in musical theater, is a natural harmony singer, so singing with her is easy. It takes a little rehearsal time but not much." Lyons has a routine to preserve his voice: "I start my day with coffee, then I have a glass of orange juice. After that, I drink a pot of decaffeinated cinnamon apple tea with honey and drink a lot of water."

In October 2013, Lyons' son Jonathan joined him onstage for the first time: "It was a Motorola employee party in Schaumburg, Illinois. Jonathan sang a lot as a kid, but through his voice change, he stopped. When his voice finally settled, it turned out to be so low, and he wasn't happy. He could no longer sing all the songs that featured high voices. His uncle Jonny was the first to ask him to try a Johnny Cash song. Jonathan didn't know Cash at the time but gave it a try, and it sounded great. I told him, 'I'll add you to my show.' Coaxing him wasn't too hard, but at the time, he was not a front guy. He wasn't sure he wanted to be either. He was a drummer in a local hard rock band and seemed to like it. However, he buckled down and learned all the popular Johnny Cash songs. It wasn't long before he decided that in order to do it right, he had to play the guitar too. He took lessons and learned. We realized that

Johnny needed a June, and Peggy was the obvious choice. That's how she became a regular in the show. She sings and runs sound.

"I thought Elvis and Cash would be a slam dunk to book, but it proved to be a harder sell than I anticipated. A lot of [promoters and club owners] just couldn't see the two performing together. My version of the show was not where each performer did a set: I wanted both to be on stage at the same time. Each would take their turn performing their hit songs while the other sang backup. Eventually, my vision gained momentum, and now it's our most popular show."

Their other production, *Elvis Through the Years*, is also well received: "Jonathan liked the fact that Elvis was a singer with a bit more animation since Johnny is stuck behind the microphone. He decided to learn the younger Elvis music to complement my concert era. We debuted at Elvis night for the Windy City Thunderbirds, a minor league baseball team in Crestwood, Illinois. From there, we decided to put together a theater show called *Elvis Through the Years*. It features both eras of Elvis along with a slideshow and narration from Peggy. She also sings harmonies. We [premiered] at the White Pines Theater in Oregon, Illinois. The show sold out so fast that they ended up adding another and then another. We now have a family music business with options."

Jonathan Lyons has found success on his own as both an Elvis Tribute Artist and a Johnny Cash Tribute Artist and fronting his own band, Jonny Lyons and the Pride. In May 2021, he issued his first CD, *A Little Somethin' Somethin,'* which features 16 original tracks.

Besides being passionate about performing, John Lyons loves meeting his fans: "Everybody has a story, and some are pretty interesting. I played several shows for a lady who was in the movie *Double Trouble* with Elvis. Another fan told me he served with Elvis in the Army. I've met others who were fortunate enough to have caught a scarf at an Elvis concert. One lady wears hers whenever she comes to our shows."

Lyons acknowledged, "My shows are for the audience, so I enjoy talking to the fans and posing for photos. Elvis fans are the best."

Garry Wesley

Three of the first Elvis Tribute Artists were Johnny Spence, Johnny Harra and Rick Saucedo. Garry Wesley got his start a bit later, in 1980. He thought dressing up as Elvis for Halloween that year would be a one-time occurrence, but it turned into a career. Today, he often

Seven. "Walk a Mile in My Shoes"

performs alongside his wife Elaine, who pays tribute to Patsy Cline. In 2013, Wesley was inducted into the International ETA Hall of Fame in Memphis and received the Heart of the King Lifetime Achievement Award in Las Vegas.

Growing up, Wesley would only sing in the church choir on Sundays and with his father at family gatherings: "My father was a huge influence because he sang and played guitar and accordion."[14] His parents loved country music, but his dad also enjoyed playing polkas. Frankie Yankovic once brought Wesley's father on stage to play accordion for him.

At age six, Wesley became an Elvis Presley fan. He ardently listened to his older brother's records and watched Presley on television. As soon as Wesley heard "Jailhouse Rock," he started dancing. His brother eventually gave him his 45 RPM record collection. In 1977, when Wesley was 17, he had a chance meeting with the King of Rock and Roll: "When Elvis traveled through Green Bay, Wisconsin, after a concert in Stevens Point, Wisconsin, his limo pulled up next to me at a stoplight. The back window came down halfway and Elvis chuckled at hearing his voice boom from my tape deck—'All Shook

Garry Wesley briefly met Elvis Presley at a red light in Green Bay, Wisconsin. Elvis' limo pulled up next to Wesley, its back window rolled halfway down, and they quickly exchanged hellos before Presley went on his way (courtesy Garry Wesley).

Up' was playing. We said hello [to one another], and Elvis said, 'How ya doing, son? You be careful!' Then the limo pulled away. I nearly had a heart attack."

On October 31, 1980, Wesley dressed up as Presley and attended a costume party at Nick's Nicabob in Milwaukee, Wisconsin, with a couple of friends who went as The Blues Brothers. Wesley went all-out to look the part. He had his hair, eyebrows and eyelashes dyed, had his hair styled, and had his sister assist with his makeup. Wesley wore a black shirt, black pants with an eagle-buckled belt and a jacket. The bouncer thought he was part of the band and chastised him for his lateness. The Rockin' Robins were the entertainment for the evening. Wesley recalled, "The band leader, Jerry, was a friend who didn't recognize me and invited me on stage to sing. [Wesley sang a medley of Presley tunes.] I was a hit." By the end of the night, Wesley was offered a regular gig at the club.

To hone his tribute, Wesley constantly practiced and even was serenaded to sleep by Presley's recordings. His friend Linda ran a theater and allowed him to come in after-hours to watch all of Presley's movies and concert footage. In the 1980s, Wesley played at Nick's Nicabob at least one weekend a month. He had another regular gig at the Vegas Club in nearby Brookfield, Wisconsin. Wesley recalled, "I ended up making more money performing as Elvis than I did at three part-time jobs."[15] After he formed his own band, the gigs increased. Wesley was so popular that in the '80s and early '90s he had a fan club. It cost $10 to join, and its perks included a photo and a newsletter every three months.

In 1992, Wesley began working with the Las Vegas production *American Super Stars.* He stayed with them for five years. He was hired by *Legends in Concert* seven years later, and worked with them on and off until 2003. Via those experiences, Wesley learned how to produce his own tribute shows: "I knew the dedication and hard work involved in putting together a production. My secret was to pick the best tribute artists and then let them choose their own material to sing, which was usually three songs each. Every tribute artist knows their abilities and which songs make them shine."

These days, Wesley is most frequently employed by casinos, theaters and festivals. Alfred's on Beale in Memphis, where he's played annually since 1988, is like a second home to him: "I had sent a video to them, and the manager loved it and hired me. I have hundreds of fans from all over the world that come to see me there during Elvis Week."

Seven. "Walk a Mile in My Shoes"

His show averages one to two hours in length. "I try to pick and include the most notable songs Elvis did, such as 'Suspicious Minds,' 'An American Trilogy' and 'My Way.' My favorites to sing are 'Hurt,' 'How Great Thou Art,' 'Suspicious Minds,' 'An American Trilogy' and 'Jailhouse Rock.' These are only a few of Elvis' signature songs that showcase his vocal versatility and power. I rarely get a request for an Elvis song that I don't know, but the lyrics are tricky. If I haven't done the song, then I will have someone pull up the lyrics on their phone and I'll read them as I sing."

One of Wesley's most successful endeavors occurred in August 2002, when the South American country Chile hosted him and fellow ETA Travis LeDoyt. Also, on the trip, too, were Presley's original drummer D.J. Fontana and a member of Presley's Memphis Mafia, Joe Esposito. Five million TV viewers tuned in to their first show. Weskey was part of two other shows performed in and around Santiago. In 2003, he won the Tribute to the King competition in Lula, Mississippi, and was awarded the largest prize ever given to an ETA, $50,000. He sang "Suspicious Minds," "Hurt" and "Can't Help Falling in Love." Wesley acknowledged, "We were allowed an eight-minute window to perform, and my song choices fit perfectly within that [amount of time]. I was surprised [to win]. I had been hopeful, but you never know what a judge is hearing and seeing."

Two thousand thirteen was a banner year for Wesley with two major accolades: induction into the International ETA Hall of Fame and recipent of the Heart of the King Lifetime Achievement Award. Regarding the latter, he admitted, "It was one of the most memorable experiences of my career as D.J. Fontana handed me my award." The ceremony was held in Las Vegas at the Westgate Hotel (formerly the International Hilton). On the same stage where Presley had entertained thousands of fans, Wesley gave his own concert. He even used the same dressing room as Presley. "The sound was amazing, and as I sang, I thought about standing in Elvis' spotlight. I was incredibly honored and so grateful to be able to pay tribute to Elvis."

Wesley's favorite aspects of being an Elvis Tribute Artist are getting to know the people Presley worked with and called his friends, meeting the fans who adored Presley, and traveling around the world to places he would never have gone if not for his love of Presley and his music: "It has been my honor to pay tribute to a man who gave so much to the world, and I hope that wherever he is, he thinks I've done him proud."[16]

You Sound Just Like...

Jay Dupuis

While Elvis Presley was alive, a few guys were already impersonating him, including Johnny Harra and Andy Kaufman. After Presley's passing, the term "impersonator" took on a negative connotation. To the public, it meant a fat guy in a badly tailored jumpsuit and a poorly fitted wig going around saying, "Thank ya, thank ya very much." Eventually, the moniker "tribute artist" was adopted. However, Jay Dupuis will admit, "I'm not an Elvis Tribute Artist. I am an Elvis impersonator, all the way. A tribute is putting your own spin on Elvis, whereas I'm actually trying to completely recreate Elvis. That's why I am so particularly [detail-conscious]. I wear the exact rings and jumpsuit from a particular concert, sing the same setlist, perform the same moves, and try to say the same things."[17] His spot-on authentic portrayal paid off. He won the Ultimate Elvis Tribute Artist Contest in 2014.

At three years old, Dupuis started singing "Hound Dog": "My mom said she played it for me, and I just got so excited. My eyes lit up, and I started dancing. I begged her to play it over and over again. For the next year or so, she said she just had to keep playing it for me. I asked for it every day." Even though his mom wasn't a big Elvis fan, she purchased every album, movie, concert and book that she could find: "I watched him every day." *This Is Elvis*, *Aloha from Hawaii*, and *That's the Way It Is* were the most frequently viewed. Unknowingly, Dupuis was studying Elvis by watching his concerts: "It became an addiction. I had to get my Elvis fix."

Dupuis has played drums professionally since age four: "My dad had a gospel group, and I played drums in it. I did a lot of studio recordings with several different artists too." Dupuis' musical influences are Presley, Tom Jones, Michael Jackson, KISS and his father: "My dad is one of the greatest male singers I've ever heard." Dupuis and his dad have even shared the stage: "He has sung harmony with me on 'Gentle on My Mind.'"

It wasn't until 2008 that Dupuis began to aspire to become a tribute artist: "When I was a kid, I'd dress up and perform for my friends and family in the living room. My mom would put on *Aloha from Hawaii* and I'd act like I was Elvis. That was just me, being a kid. Then I kind of moved away from Elvis because to other kids, Elvis wasn't cool. I came back to him in my early thirties, in 2008. My dad asked me to sing an Elvis song for his birthday party on Christmas Eve, so I sang 'C.C. Rider.' He [was surprised] because I didn't sing any more. My dad is an

Seven. "Walk a Mile in My Shoes"

Jay Dupuis admits that he is not a tribute artist but an impersonator because he tries hard to recreate Elvis Presley. He is very particular in replicating specific jumpsuits and setlists. His attention to detail helped him secure the title of the Ultimate Elvis in 2014 (courtesy Jay Dupuis).

amazing singer, but I was always so shy to sing in front of him. I wasn't in his class, and I never wanted him to say anything [like], 'You're okay.'"

Dupuis added, "It was a large party with a lot of family members in attendance. Everybody really liked it. It renewed my love for Elvis. Then the following year, I went to B&K [Enterprises Costume Company] and I bought a professional jumpsuit and a professional wig. I performed for my dad's birthday again."

In 2010, Dupuis entered his first contest. The day after he placed third at the Ultimate, he received a call from the owner of the largest theater in Pigeon Forge, Tennessee, with an offer to be his full-time Presley: "That's how my career started."

The King in Concert debuted in 2012: "That is a special show. During my career, that's one of the highlights. Presley Productions, now RRAM Artist Agency, had put on a festival called the EP Expo, and they wanted me to do a *That's the Way It Is* show for them. They were going to have guest speakers—Joe Guercio, Sam Thompson and The Imperials. Joe was also going to front a 20-piece orchestra along with the EAS Band." Dupuis accepted the offer. When it came to rehearsals, he did his portion and then sat in the audience to watch the others. "Joe was teaching the orchestra how to play 'Also Sprach Zarathustra,' then said, 'All right, I need to teach you guys how to do 'Just Pretend.' He told them, 'I used to love performing this song with Elvis. At the end of the song, I'd be directing the orchestra to do something, and I'd turn around, and Elvis would be doing something different with the band. We'd look at each other and smile. That was our moment.' Then he said, 'We need a singer. Is there somebody that can come up and sing this song?' The director said to me, 'Jay, you're right there. Can you come up and sing this song? You're gonna be the one singing it [tonight].' I was nervous because The Imperials and Joe Guercio are there, and they also had a couple of Elvis' horn players in the orchestra. I hadn't warmed up or anything, and 'Just Pretend' is not an easy song, but I finished the song and walked offstage. Terry Blackwood of The Imperials came up to where I was seated and said, 'You're not one of those guys who walk around with the sideburns and stuff like that.' I said, 'No, I'm just me. I'm kind of like an actor. I put on all that stuff [makeup, wig, sideburns and jumpsuit] while I'm on stage to try and recreate Elvis, but then I walk offstage and I'm little ol' me again.' He said, 'I like that. You mind if we sing with you tonight?' I was like, 'What?' He repeated, 'We'd like to join you on stage tonight since you're an actor, and you're only trying to act like Elvis.' I replied, 'That would be amazing!'

Seven. "Walk a Mile in My Shoes"

"I came back on stage to sing another song, and Joe walked over to The Imperials. Then they had a little meeting and invited me in. They said, 'Hey, we're gonna get into trouble with the other band members, but we'd like to perform with you. You'll be the first [ETA] that we ever do this with.' After that, they said, 'We'd like to do this tour with you.'" The production still takes place sometimes, just not as often, and Guercio (who died in 2015) is no longer a part of it. Blackwood later told Dupuis, "You know, out of all these guys we've heard do this, you actually have Elvis' tone. That's what made us want to sing with you. When you close your eyes, you sound so much like Elvis."

In 2013, Dupuis teamed with *Legends in Concert*: "Leo Days had to miss a week of work in Myrtle Beach [South Carolina] and they needed an Elvis. Leo [had told them], 'Hey, look, this guy Jay that I know, he's pretty good. He could probably do it.' I came and filled in for him for nine days. Six months later, they called me back to do a whole season with them. When I won the Ultimate, they paraded me around to all of the [cities]. They really work you quite a bit. Every couple of years, I still do a season." In 2019, their Garth Brooks tribute artist couldn't perform one evening, so Dupuis did a 45-minute set: "Normally, I sing eight songs: 'C.C. Rider,' 'Hound Dog,' 'You Gave Me a Mountain,' 'I Can't Stop Loving You,' 'Blue Suede Shoes,' 'Kentucky Rain,' 'Suspicious Minds' and 'Can't Help Falling in Love.' Those songs have varied over the years."

As far as choosing setlists for his own shows, he says it all depends on who hires him and what they are hiring him for. If they want a recreation of one of Presley's Madison Square Garden shows, he goes to elvis-concerts.com, seeks out the setlist and jumpsuit then does it. Some of his favorites to sing are "Just Pretend," "Suspicious Minds" and "If I Can Dream." Dupuis stated, "I love the studio version of 'Suspicious Minds.' You can hear the emotion in his voice when he's singing it. 'If I Can Dream' really means something special to me. This was a dream when I was a young child to perform as Elvis. Every time I sing 'If I Can Dream,' at the very end, I lift my hands up and say, 'Thank you, Jesus, for allowing me to do this.'"

The year 2013 marked his second attempt at winning the Ultimate. Dean Z won that year, and Dupuis was second. The following year, Dupuis returned in the hopes that 2014 would be his time to shine. He admitted that it's a process to get to the finals: "You have to turn in a list of 20 songs to Elvis Presley Enterprises. Then [for the competition], they choose your songs off that list. After the first round, where you sing two songs (mine were 'Suspicious Minds' and 'You Don't Have to Say You Love Me'), they choose the Top Ten. Then you sing two more songs to get to the Top Five. If you're in the Top Five, you get to choose what you want to sing, from your list.

"After the first round, I got to meet the judges. They were asking me questions, so I said, 'Can I ask you a question?'" Dupuis proceeded to ask them what qualified them to judge him in this competition. Two of the ladies had worked extensively as producers on *Prince from Another Planet*, which featured Presley at Madison Square Garden in 1972.

"Going into the second round, I was hoping that I would get something decent. The last song on my list was 'Proud Mary,' and that's just a throwaway. However, that song and 'Never Been to Spain' were what EPE chose for me. I was like, 'Great,' but then all of a sudden, it dawned on me that Elvis performed those back to back at Madison Square Garden, wearing the Wheat suit and cape. I walked out in that replica suit and cape. No one had ever worn a cape in the Ultimate. The judges said, 'You nailed it. You won the contest for us in the second round. As soon as you walked out in that suit, we recognized it.' I had used their knowledge to my advantage. In the final round, I chose 'Polk Salad Annie,' and I won." Dupuis was awarded a *Legends in Concert* contract, an Ultimate ETA Contest belt and $20,000. Incidentally, voting criteria was based upon vocals which counted for 40 percent, and appearance, stage presence, and overall performance, which counted for 20 percent each.

The Wheat suit may have won him the competition crown, but his favorite jumpsuit is the Chain. Dupuis revealed, "All my suits come from B&K. You can't beat 'em. They basically took over the company from Bill Belew and Gene Doucette, the people who made Elvis' costumes. B&K has all the original patterns [and use them to make the ones today]. If you get a suit with embroidery, Gene Doucette still does it." From 1972 to 1977, Doucette created all of Presley's jumpsuits because Belew was too busy working on other projects.

"I'm really, really particular about my jumpsuits. For example, I ordered a new Aloha suit, and I wanted it exactly like the one used in the television special. [There were two suits—one designed for the January 12, 1973, rehearsal show and then a completely different suit was used for the main show.] B&K had reproduced the rehearsal suit for so many years, but with me studying all this stuff and being so particular, I decided I wanted the main suit. There are differences in the design of the eagle and where certain stars are placed. There were also two variations of capes. The first cape had blue studs that showcased the design on the eagle wings, while the other had gold, so there was no depth to the design." Incidentally, Doucette said he couldn't stand the gold-studded cape. Dupuis commented, "They had never used that jumpsuit pattern [for any ETA], but they made it for me."

Dupuis continued, "My body and Elvis' body are completely different. Elvis had broad shoulders, a thin waist, and really skinny legs. The most he weighed for *Aloha* was 165 lbs. He only weighed 155 for *That's the Way It Is*. My body can't get that small. I have a lot more muscle tone than Elvis had. I get my suits cut a certain way, so my body can look like that. I get my shoulders wider, and it's tighter around my belly."

By 2014, Dupuis was also a regular member of *Elvis Lives*, a production developed by *Legends in Concert* and Elvis Presley Enterprises: "In 2013, Leo Days had to miss a couple of days, so they brought me in to do his part. The producers came to me and said, 'We want you to be a part of *Elvis Lives*, but we really need you to win this contest.' I said, 'I'm gonna do whatever I can. I'll do my best.' They told me, 'No, really, really do your best because we want it to be called the *Ultimate Elvis Tribute Artists Concert—Elvis Lives*.' That would mean that all three of us would be Ultimates, and they never had that before. As soon as I won, they had the contract in front of me. Dean Z had told the tour manager, 'This is the right combination. We need to get Jay.'" Dupuis participated in its run from 2014 to 2017. During the majority of that time, Dean Z and Bill Cherry were also part of the production. According to Dupuis, "In the beginning, Bill Cherry was my mentor. The first time he saw me perform in a contest, he said, 'I'd like to steer your path, so you can become an Ultimate. I'd like to help you as much as I can.' We became close friends." In recent years, Dupuis has paid it forward and returned the favor by providing guidance to some of the up-and-coming ETAs, such as Cote Deonath.

Dupuis considers being an Elvis Tribute Artist a true blessing and he is honored to pay tribute to Elvis, whom he calls "the greatest entertainer of all-time."[18] He added, "It's amazing how one man has affected so many people."

Chapter Notes

Chapter One

1. Kavan Hashemian, email interview by Sheree Homer, 14 August 2019. All quotes that follow are from the same interview, unless otherwise noted.
2. Travis LeDoyt, email interview by Sheree Homer, 6 September 2019. All quotes that follow are from the same interview, unless otherwise noted.
3. Caden Gamblin, email interview by Sheree Homer, 6 September 2019. All quotes that follow are from the same interview, unless otherwise noted.
4. Carolyn MacArthur, "Great Upcoming Contest and Show," *Sideburns Magazine*, https://carolyn-macarthur.squarespace.com/blog?offset=1552081438274, accessed December 20, 2020.
5. Ricky Aron, email interview by Sheree Homer, 11 September 2019. All quotes that follow are from the same interview, unless otherwise noted.
6. Jake Slater, email interview by Sheree Homer, 22 October 2019. All quotes that follow are from the same interview, unless otherwise noted.
7. Carolyn MacArthur, "Focus On: ETA Jake Slater and Laura West," *Sideburns Magazine*, https://www.sideburnsmagazine.com/focus-on-blog/2019/9/8/focus-on-eta-jake-slater-and-laura-west, accessed June 5, 2021.
8. Finley Watkins, email interview by Sheree Homer, 6 September 2019. All quotes that follow are from the same interview, unless otherwise noted.
9. "Bio," Finley Watkins Official Homepage, https://finleywatkins.com/bio, accessed June 1, 2021.

Chapter Two

1. Johnny Rogers, email interview by Sheree Homer, 7 September 2019. All quotes that follow are from the same interview, unless otherwise noted.
2. "Johnny Rogers: Legends of Country," Wildey Theatre, http://www.wildeytheatre.com/?nav=eventsDetails&num=532, accessed September 9, 2021.
3. Marlys Barker, "Johnny Rogers' Legends of Country Show Coming to Talent Factory," *Ames Tribune*, https://www.amestrib.com/entertainment/20190202/-johnny-rogers8217-legends-of-country-show-coming-to-talent-factory, accessed September 9, 2021.
4. John Mueller, email interview by Sheree Homer, Mueller, John. 23 September 2019. All quotes that follow are from the same interview, unless otherwise noted.
5. Andy Gregurich, "Ooh-Wee-Ooh, I Live Just Like Buddy Holly," *The Outline*, https://theoutline.com/post/7371/-buddy-holly-john-mueller-interview, accessed September 29, 2021.

Chapter Three

1. Luke Stroud, email interview by Sheree Homer, 1 September 2019. All quotes that follow are from the same interview, unless otherwise noted.
2. Patty Thayer, "*Million Dollar Quartet*: A Whole Lot of Rockin' Going On!," *San Luis Obispo Rep*, https://www.slorep.org/million-dollar-quartet-a-whole-lot-of-rockin-going-on/, accessed October 11, 2021.
3. Jared Freiburg, email interview by

Notes—Chapter Four

Sheree Homer, 3 September 2019. All quotes that follow are from the same interview, unless otherwise noted.

4. Doug Cooke, email interview by Sheree Homer, 23 August 2019. All quotes that follow are from the same interview, unless otherwise noted.

5. Jacob Tolliver, phone interview by Sheree Homer, 26 August 2019. All quotes that follow are from the same interview, unless otherwise noted.

6. Shawna Hudson, "Here's the Full Lowdown on Jacob Tolliver," Sweety High, https://www.sweetyhigh.com/read/jacob-tolliver-music-mcm-facts-120318, accessed November 8, 2021.

Chapter Four

1. Al Jackson, Email Interview By Sheree Homer, 26 August 2019. All quotes that follow are from the same interview, unless otherwise noted.

2. Jesse Aron, email interview by Sheree Homer, 23 September 2019. All quotes that follow are from the same interview, unless otherwise noted.

3. Carolyn MacArthur, "Spotlight On: ETA Jesse Aron," *Sideburns Magazine*, https://www.sideburnsmagazine.com/blog/2020/9/15/spotlight-on-eta-jesse-aaron, accessed August 26, 2021.

4. *Ibid*.

5. Rick Lindy, email interview by Sheree Homer, 8 December 2019. All quotes that follow are from the same interview, unless otherwise noted.

6. Lottie Elizabeth Johnson, "Inside the Life of a Little Richard Impersonator," *Deseret News*, https://www.deseret.com/entertainment/2020/5/23/21266266/-little-richard-death-funeral-alabama-richard-penniman-garry-moore-hawaii-impersonator?fbclid=IwAR0Uz8bei2wQJMY4-0vAsZiUG0KQJ_taEJqBTt8H4NRtsVH_6cSscV_LckQ, accessed June 23, 2020.

7. Garry Moore, email interview by Sheree Homer, 27 August 2019. All quotes that follow are from the same interview, unless otherwise noted.

8. Lottie Elizabeth Johnson, "Inside the Life of a Little Richard Impersonator," *Deseret News*, https://www.deseret.com/entertainment/2020/5/23/21266266/little-richard-death-funeral-alabama-richard-penniman-garry-moore-hawaii-impersonator?fbclid=IwAR0Uz8bei2wQJMY4-0vAsZiUG0KQJ_taEJqBTt8H4NRtsVH_6cSscV_LckQ, accessed June 23, 2020.

9. "Garry Moore Biography," Impersonators Central, http://celebrity-look alikes.com/performers/gmemcee.htm, accessed March 3, 2020.

10. David Bogle, email interview by Sheree Homer, 12 August 2019. All quotes that follow are from the same interview, unless otherwise noted.

11. Scott Hinds, email interview by Sheree Homer, 16 August 2019. All quotes that follow are from the same interview, unless otherwise noted.

12. Steve Wildsmith, "A Doggone Good Time: The Royal Hounds Spice Up Their Rockabilly with Some Onstage Insanity," *The Daily Times*, https://www.thedailytimes.com/entertainment/a-doggone-good-time-the-royal-hounds-spice-up-their-rockabilly-with-some-onstage-insanity/article_812c5f26-cf89-52fb-9031-46c1bc14d9aa.html, accessed October 1, 2021.

13. Ty Stone, email interview by Sheree Homer, 7 October 2019. All quotes that follow are from the same interview, unless otherwise noted.

14. C.J., "James Brown Impersonator Feels Good About His Model," *Star Tribune*, https://www.startribune.com/c-j-james-brown-impersonator-feels-good-about-his-model/367038631/, accessed October 17, 2021.

15. John Reinan, "Bloomington Man Channels Soul Brother No. 1 with James Brown Tribute Show," *Star Tribune*, https://www.startribune.com/bloomington-man-channels-soul-brother-no-1-with-james-brown-tribute-show/331616592/, accessed October 17, 2021.

16. Pete Hutton, email interview by Sheree Homer, 11 December 2019. All quotes that follow are from the same interview, unless otherwise noted.

Notes—Chapters Five, Six and Seven

Chapter Five

1. Tammi Savoy, email interview by Sheree Homer, 31 August 2019. All quotes that follow are from the same interview, unless otherwise noted.
2. Jack Watkins, "The Tammi Show," *Vintage Rock Magazine*, Feb/March 2021, 55.
3. Ken Burke, "'Rhythm and Roll' Chris Casello Returns... with Miss Tammi Savoy," *Blue Suede News*, Summer 2018, 10.
4. Bee Townsend, "Interview with Tammi Savoy," *Vintage Woman Magazine*, https://thevintagewomanmagazine.com/interview-with-tammi-savoy/, accessed August 5, 2021.
5. Julie Myers, email interview by Sheree Homer, 27 August 2019. All quotes that follow are from the same interview, unless otherwise noted.
6. Markos Papadatos, "Interview: Julie C. Myers Talks Stevie Nicks and 'Nearly Nicks,'" Digital Journal, https://www.digitaljournal.com/entertainment/interview-julie-c-myers-talks-stevie-nicks-and-nearly-nicks/article/425075, accessed October 10, 2021.
7. Laura West, email interview by Sheree Homer, 19 October 2019. All quotes that follow are from the same interview, unless otherwise noted.
8. Herman Fuselier, "Cher Impersonator Will Make You Dance," *The Daily Advertiser*, https://www.theadvertiser.com/story/entertainment/music/2015/06/10/cher-impersonator-will-make-dance/71009548/, accessed October 28, 2021.
9. Lisa Irion, email interview by Sheree Homer, 15 August 2019. All quotes that follow are from the same interview, unless otherwise noted.
10. "Tribute Artist- Amberley Beatty," Fusion Talent Group, http://www.fusiontalentgroup.com/entertainers/-amberley-beatty, accessed October 26, 2021.
11. Amberley Beatty, email interview by Sheree Homer, 22 September 2019. All quotes that follow are from the same interview, unless otherwise noted.
12. Elaine Wesley, email interview by Sheree Homer, 9 September 2019. All quotes that follow are from the same interview, unless otherwise noted.

Chapter Six

1. Zach McNabb, phone interview by Sheree Homer, 4 October 2021. All quotes that follow are from the same interview, unless otherwise noted.
2. Pete Storm, email interview by Sheree Homer, 26 August 2019. All quotes that follow are from the same interview, unless otherwise noted.
3. Christopher Essex, email interview by Sheree Homer, 17 November 2019. All quotes that follow are from the same interview, unless otherwise noted.
4. Justin Loretangeli, "Christopher J. Essex Introduces Himself with Rockabilly Single 'Swipe Right on Me,'" Pro Country Music, https://procountrymusic.com/2020/11/02/christopher-j-essex-introduces-himself-with-rockabilly-single-swipe-right-on-me/, accessed May 21, 2021.
5. Patti McClintic, "Riveting Interview with Country's New Rising Star Christopher J. Essex," Think Country, https://thinkcountrymusic.com/whats-new/riveting-interview-with-countrys-new-rising-star-christopher-j-essex/, accessed May 21, 2021.

Chapter Seven

1. Leo Days, email interview by Sheree Homer, 19 August 2019. All quotes that follow are from the same interview, unless otherwise noted.
2. "Local Impresonators Keep Elvis Alive for Fans Around the World," *Tri-County Times*, https://www.tctimes.com/living/local-impresonators-keep-elvis-alive-for-fans-around-the-world/-article_edd7b8b8-e2b5-11e3-a766-0019bb2963f4.html, accessed August 15, 2021.
3. Doug Church, email interview by Sheree Homer, 13 August 2019. All quotes that follow are from the same interview, unless otherwise noted.
4. Simran Khurana, "Quotes About

Notes—Chapter Seven

Elvis Presley," Thought Co., https://www.thoughtco.com/quotes-about-elvis-presley-2833517, accessed September 25, 2021.

5. Sally Friedman, "Doug Church Brings Elvis Back to Life at Sunnybrook," *The Mercury*, https://www.pottsmerc.com/arts_and_entertainment/doug-church-brings-elvis-back-to-life-at-sunnybrook/article_174450a7-85f0-5094-a2b9-541edd2ad200.html, accessed September 25, 2021.

6. Michael St. Angel, email interview by Sheree Homer, 16 August 2019. All quotes that follow are from the same interview, unless otherwise noted.

7. Gib Maynard, email interview by Sheree Homer, 7 September 2019. All quotes that follow are from the same interview, unless otherwise noted.

8. Bill Cherry, email interview by Sheree Homer, 6 September 2019. All quotes that follow are from the same interview, unless otherwise noted.

9. Ted Torres Martin, email interview by Sheree Homer, 4 September 2019. All quotes that follow are from the same interview, unless otherwise noted.

10. Johnny Thompson, email interview by Sheree Homer, 23 September 2019. All quotes that follow are from the same interview, unless otherwise noted.

11. Tracy Watler, "One Elvis Tribute Artist Has East Texas Connection," KLTV, https://www.kltv.com/story/6698652/one-elvis-tribute-artist-has-east-texas-connection/, accessed September 27, 2021.

12. Dwight Icenhower, email interview by Sheree Homer, 6 September 2019. All quotes that follow are from the same interview, unless otherwise noted.

13. John Lyons, email interview by Sheree Homer, 31 August 2019. All quotes that follow are from the same interview, unless otherwise noted.

14. Garry Wesley, email interview by Sheree Homer, 9 September 2019. All quotes that follow are from the same interview, unless otherwise noted.

15. Carolyn MacArthur, "Focus On: ETA Garry Wesley, the Early Years," *Sideburns Magazine*, https://www.sideburnsmagazine.com/focus-on-blog-2/2020/5/10/focus-on-eta-garry-wesley-the-early-years, accessed November 2, 2021.

16. "ETA Spotlight- Garry Wesley," Lady Luck Music, http://www.ladyluckmusic.com/radio/etaspotlight/garrywesley/, accessed November 2, 2021.

17. Jay Dupuis, phone interview by Sheree Homer, 23 September 2019. All quotes that follow are from the same interview, unless otherwise noted.

18. "Biography," Jay Dupuis Official Homepage, https://www.jaydupuisaselvis.com/bio, accessed November 5, 2021.

Bibliography

Interviews by the Author

Aron, Jesse. 23 September 2019.
Aron, Ricky. 11 September 2019.
Beatty, Amberley. 22 September 2019.
Bogle, David. 12 August 2019.
Cherry, Bill. 6 September 2019.
Church, Doug. 13 August 2019.
Cooke, Doug. 23 August 2019.
Days, Leo. 19 August 2019.
Dupuis, Jay. 23 September 2019.
Essex, Christopher. 17 November 2019.
Freiburg, Jared. 7 September 2019.
Gamblin, Caden. 6 September 2019.
Hashemian, Kavan. 14 August 2019.
Hinds, Scott. 16 August 2019.
Hutton, Pete. 11 December 2019.
Icenhower, Dwight. 6 September 2019.
Irion, Lisa. 15 August 2019.
Jackson, Al. 26 August 2019.
LeDoyt, Travis. 6 September 2019.
Lindy, Rick. 8 December 2019.
Lyons, John. 31 August 2019.
Martin Torres, Ted. 4 September 2019.
Maynard, Gib. 7 September 2019.
McNabb, Zach. 4 October 2021.
Moore, Garry. 27 August 2019.
Mueller, John. 23 September 2019.
Myers, Julie. 27 August 2019.
Rogers, Johnny. 7 September 2019.
St. Angel, Michael. 16 August 2019.
Savoy, Tammi. 31 August 2019.
Slater, Jake. 22 October 2019.
Stone, Ty. 7 October 2019.
Storm, Pete. 26 August 2019.
Stroud, Luke. 1 September 2019.
Thompson, Johnny. 23 September 2019.
Tolliver, Jacob. 26 August 2019.
Watkins, Finley. 6 September 2019.
Wesley, Elaine. 9 September 2019.
Wesley, Garry. 9 September 2019.
West, Laura. 19 October 2019.

Periodicals

Burke, Ken. "'Rhythm and Roll' Chris Casello Returns... with Miss Tammi Savoy." *Blue Suede News* (Summer 2018): 10–11.
Watkins, Jack. "The Tammi Show." *Vintage Rock Magazine* (Feb/March 2021): 54–57.

Websites

Barker, Marlys. https://www.amestrib.com/entertainment/20190202/johnny-rogers8217-legends-of-country-show-coming-to-talent-factory, accessed September 9, 2021.
C.J. https://www.startribune.com/c-j-james-brown-impersonator-feels-good-about-his-model/367038631/, accessed October 17, 2021.
Finley Watkins Official Homepage. https://finleywatkins.com/bio, accessed June 1, 2021.
Friedman, Sally. https://www.pottsmerc.com/arts_and_entertainment/doug-church-brings-elvis-back-to-life-at-sunnybrook/article_174450a7-85f0-5094-a2b9-541edd2ad200.html, accessed September 25, 2021.
Fuselier, Herman. https://www.theadvertiser.com/story/entertainment/music/2015/06/10/cher-impersonator-will-make-dance/71009548/, accessed October 28, 2021.
Fusion Talent Group. http://www.fusiontalentgroup.com/entertainers/-amberley-beatty, accessed October 26, 2021.
Gregurich, Andy. https://theoutline.com/post/7371/buddy-holly-john-mueller-interview, accessed September 29, 2021.

Bibliography

Hudson, Shawna. https://www.sweetyhigh.com/read/jacob-tolliver-music-mcm-facts-120318, accessed November 8, 2021.

Impersonators Central. http://celebritylookalikes.com/performers/gmemcee.htm, accessed March 3, 2020.

Jay Dupuis Official Homepage. https://www.jaydupuisaselvis.com/bio, accessed November 5, 2021.

Johnson, Lottie Elizabeth. https://www.deseret.com/entertainment/2020/5/23/21266266/little-richard-death-funeral-alabama-richard-penniman-garry-moore-hawaii-impersonator?fbclid=IwAR0Uz8bei2wQJMY4-0vAsZiUG0KQJ_taEJqBTt8H4NRtsVH_6cSscV_LckQ, accessed June 23, 2020.

Khurana, Simran. https://www.thoughtco.com/quotes-about-elvis-presley-2833517, accessed September 25, 2021.

Lady Luck Music. http://www.ladyluckmusic.com/radio/etaspotlight/garrywesley/, accessed November 2, 2021.

Loretangeli, Justin. https://procountrymusic.com/2020/11/02/christopher-j-essex-introduces-himself-with-rockabilly-single-swipe-right-on-me/, accessed May 21, 2021.

MacArthur, Carolyn. https://carolynmacarthur.squarespace.com/blog?offset=1552081438274, accessed December 20, 2020.

———. Https://www.sideburnsmagazine.com/blog/2020/9/15/spotlight-on-eta-jesse-aaron, Accessed August 26, 2021.

———. https://www.sideburnsmagazine.com/focus-on-blog-2/2020/5/10/-focus-on-eta-garry-wesley-the-early-years, accessed November 2, 2021.

———. Https://www.sideburnsmagazine.com/focus-on-blog/2019/9/8/focus-on-eta-jake-slater-and-laura-west, Accessed June 5, 2021.

McClintic, Patti. https://thinkcountrymusic.com/whats-new/riveting-interview-with-countrys-new-rising-star-christopher-j-essex/, accessed May 21, 2021.

Papadatos, Markos. https://www.digitaljournal.com/entertainment/interview-julie-c-myers-talks-stevie-nicks-and-nearly-nicks/article/425075, accessed October 10, 2021.

Reinan, John. https://www.startribune.com/bloomington-man-channels-soul-brother-no-1-with-james-brown-tribute-show/331616592/, accessed October 17, 2021.

Thayer, Patty. https://www.slorep.org/-million-dollar-quartet-a-whole-lot-of-rockin-going-on/, accessed October 11, 2021.

Townsend, Bee. https://thevintagewomanmagazine.com/interview-with-tammi-savoy/, accessed January 15, 2021.

Tri- County Times. https://www.tctimes.com/living/local-impresonators-keep-elvis-alive-for-fans-around-the-world/-article_edd7b8b8-e2b5-11e3-a766-0019bb2963f4.html, accessed August 15, 2021.

Watler, Tracy. https://www.kltv.com/story/6698652/one-elvis-tribute-artist-has-east-texas-connection/, accessed September 27, 2021.

Wildey Theatre. http://www.wildeytheatre.com/?nav=eventsDetails&num=532, accessed September 9, 2021.

Wildsmith, Steve. https://www.thedailytimes.com/entertainment/-a-doggone-good-time-the-royal-hounds-spice-up-their-rockabilly-with-some-onstage-insanity/-article_812c5f26-cf89-52fb-9031-46c1bc14d9aa.html, accessed October 1, 2021.

Index

Numbers in **_bold italics_** indicate pages with illustrations

Addams, Gomez 84–85
Aerosmith 59, 87
"All Shook Up" 92, 126, 133–134
Allsup, Tommy 23, 27
Aloha from Hawaii Via Satellite 110, 136, 141
"Also Sprach Zarathustra" 131, 138
"An American Trilogy" 12, 106, 108–109, 124, 131, 135
Americana (musical genre) 60, 63, 118
Ameripolitan Awards 76–77
Andrew, Martin D. 77, 79
Ann-Margret 2, 79–81
Aron, Jesse 51–53, *52*
Aron, Ricky 14–16, *15*
Atkinson, Jon 91, 94

B&K Enterprises Costume Company 7, 14, 138, 140
"Baby Let's Play House" 18, 80
Bad Bob Vapors 106, 114
Bartholomew, Dave 50–51
Be Bop a Lula (musical) 23–26
The Beach Boys 45, 120
The Beatles 1, 3, 6, 10, 34, 57, 59, 113, 122, 126, 128–129
Beatty, Amberley 85–88, *86*
Bennett, Brandon 5, 75
Bennett, Tony 41, 45
Berry, Chuck 1,8, 21, 24, 31, 37–38, 41, 59, 129
The Beyonders 70, 72
The Big Bopper 24–25, 27
Bigtone Records 91, 94
Blackwood, Terry 138–139
"Blue Suede Shoes" 7–8, 19–20, 31, 42, 71, 93, 103, 139
"Blueberry Hill" 47, 51
blues (musical genre) 7, 29, 36, 47, 57, 63, 65, 111, 119
The Blues Brothers 69, 104, 134
Bogle, David 59–63, *61*
Brando, Marlon 54, 56
Brooks, Garth 119, 139
Brown, James 2, 59, 67–70

Bruce, Scot 37, 40
Bublé, Michael 53, 65
Buddy: The Buddy Holly Story 23, 26
Bunch, Carl 25–26
Burgess, Sonny 29–32
"Burning Love" 12, 131
Burton, James 19, 32

Cagney, James 57, 68
"Can't Help Falling in Love" 13, 96, 107, 123–125, 131, 135, 139
Carter, June 13, 55, 89, 132
Casello, Chris 73, 76
Cash, Johnny 2, 4–5, 13, 18–19, 21, 24, 29, 31, 37, 40, 53–55, 81, 84, 92–93, 95–99, 131–132
The Cash and Cline Show 81, 84
Cave City Watermelon Festival 30–32
"C.C. Rider" 107, 112–113, 131, 136, 139
Charles, Ray 33, 35, 39, 69, 73, 104, 107
Cher 2, 81–85
Cherry, Bill 4, 76, 113–116, *114*, 141
Christmas Is a Special Day (album) 46, 48
Church, Doug 104–108, *105*
Cline, Patsy 2, 54, 81, 84–89, 133
Cochran, Eddie 24, 60, 71
Como, Perry 16, 34
Connick, Harry, Jr. 33–34
Cooke, Doug 37–41, *38*
country music 2, 29, 45, 90, 92, 94, 97, 99, 112–113, 119, 133
"Crazy" 89, 93

Darin, Bobby 34, 109, 116
Davis, Sammy, Jr. 59, 116
Days, Leo 100–103, *101*, 139, 141
DeGeneres, Ellen 19–20
Deonath, Cote 79, 141
Diamond, Neil 37, 96, 122
Domino, Fats 1–2, 24, 43, 46–51, 59
Donner, Ral 70–71
Doucette, Gene 140–141
Dreams: A Classic Rock Fantasy 77, 79
Dupuis, Jay 4, 136–141, *137*

Index

Elvis Presley Enterprises 3, 114, 124–125, 139–141
Elvis Week 6–7, 19–20, 134
Essex, Christopher 97–99, *98*
The Everly Brothers 24, 118

"The Fat Man" 49, 51
Fleetwood Mac 77–79
"Folsom Prison Blues" 36, 92–93
Fontana, D.J. 9, 55, 62, 66, 116, 135
"A Fool Such as I" 17, 71
Fox, Nance 123–124
Francis, Connie 53, 85, 87–89
Freiburg, Jared 32–37, *33*
Full House 42, 44–45

Gamblin, Caden 12–14, *13*
"Ghost Riders in the Sky" 67, 96
G.I. Blues (movie) 12, 71
Gilley, Mickey 18, 31–32
gospel music 12, 29, 93, 104, 107, 111, 113, 136
Graceland 3, 79
Great Balls of Fire (movie) 30, 39
"Great Balls of Fire" (song) 31, 33–34, 36, 40, 43
Guercio, Joe 138–139

Halloween (holiday) 52–53, 101, 114, 132
"Hang Up My Rock and Roll Shoes" 30, 32
Harra, Johnny 3, 132, 136
Hashemian, Kavan 5–8, *6*
Heart of the King Lifetime Achievement Award 104, 133, 135
"Heartbreak Hotel" 12, 19, 51
Hemsby Rock and Roll Weekender 8, 11, 71
Henley, Don 78–79
"Hey Buddy" 24, 27
Hilton Hotel 118, 135
Hinds, Scott 63–67, *64*
Holland, W.S. 9, 11
Holly, Buddy 1–2, 4, 18–19, 21–28, 60–61, 93
"Hound Dog" 10, 12, 19–20, 42, 68, 93, 136, 139
"How Great Thou Art" 131, 135
Humperdinck, Engelbert 109, 122
"Hurt" (Elvis song) 51, 106, 117, 129, 131, 135
Hutton, Pete 70–72, *70*

Icenhower, Dwight 4, 125–127, *126*
"If I Can Dream" 7, 139
"If I Could Turn Back Time" 82–83
The Imperials 138–139
Intveld, James 26, 70–72
Irion, Lisa 81–85, *83*
Isaak, Chris 16, 109, 116

Jackson, Al 46–51, *46*
Jackson, Michael 34, 51, 58, 78, 103, 136
Jackson, Wanda 53, 57
Jagger, Mick 45, 77, 79
Jailhouse Rock (movie) 6, 116
"Jailhouse Rock" (song) 7–8, 121, 129, 131, 133, 135
The James Brown Experience 67, 69
Jerry Lee Lewis Ranch 31, 37, 39
"Jim Dandy" 73, 76
Joel, Billy 34, 126
John, Elton 18–19, 43, 81, 104, 125–127
"Johnny B. Goode" 15, 42–43
Jones, George 21, 86–87, 122
Jones, Tom 45, 58, 122, 136
The Jordanaires 89–90, 118
jumpsuits 7, 20, 51, 89, 96, 105, 107, 109–115, 118, 130–131, 136–140
"Just Pretend" 15, 138–139

Karl, Allen 86, 88
Kaufman, Andy 3, 136
King, B.B. 47, 67
King Creole (movie) 7, 10, 71
Kiss (rock band) 104, 136
Klush, Shawn 3, 8, 125
Knight, Gladys 67–68
Kreis, Levi 4, 97

"Landslide" 77, 79
Lansky's 7, 14
"Last Name" 121, 124
Led Zeppelin 3, 10, 34, 104
LeDoyt, Travis 8–12, *9*, 135
Legends in Concert 8, 57, 59, 78, 102–103, 106, 115, 125, 134, 139–141
Lewis, Jerry Lee 1–2, 4–5, 16, 18–21, 24, 29–45, 60, 97, 129
Lewis, Smiley 47, 51
Leyland, Carl Sonny 91, 94
Lindy, Rick 53–57, *54*
Lipinsky, Lance 20, 73, 75–76, 118
"Little Darlin'" 108–109
Little Richard 1–2, 8, 24, 31, 37–38, 43, 57–59, 129
"Love Me" 15, 104, 112
"Love Me Tender" 104, 131
The Lovettes 73, 75
"Lucille" 58–59
Lynn, Loretta 85–89
Lyons, Jessica 73, 75
Lyons, Jonathan 128, 131–132
Lyons, John 128–132, *128*
Lyons, Peggy 128, 130–132

Madison Square Garden 139–140
Madonna 85, 87, 103
Martin, Dean 16, 21, 23, 34, 96, 116, 122

Index

Martin, Ted Torres 116–120, *117*
Maynard, Gib 110–113, *111*
McDowell, Ronnie 9, 18, 104
McEntire, Reba 79, 89
McNabb, Caleb 92, 94
McNabb, Zach 91–94, *91*
Mead, Chuck 35–36
"Mean Woman Blues" 36, 95
Michigan Elvis Festival 101–102
Miller, Glenn 39, 42
Million Dollar Quartet (musical) 4, 5, 32, 34, 36, 42, 44, 63–65, 97–99
The Monkees 128–129
Monroe, Marilyn 53, 79–81
Montage (rock band) 128–129
Moore, Garry 57–59, *58*
Moore, Scotty 9, 19, 62
Moroko, Johnny 77, 79
Morrow, Neil 12, 37, 39–40
Motown Records 57, 73
MTV 123–124
Mueller, George 24, 27
Mueller, John 23–28, *25*
The Music Man 54, 97
"My Way" 106, 108–109, 115, 125, 135
Myers, Julie 77–79, *77*

Nearly Nicks 77–78
Nelson, Rick 1–2, 4, 16, 21, 53, 59–62, 70–72, 118, 126
Nelson, Willie 29, 55, 107
Nicks, Stevie 2, 77–79

"Oh What a Price" 46, 48
One Night in Memphis 27, 32
Orbison, Roy 2, 4, 12–13, 21, 29, 51–54, 56, 116, 126

Painter, Alan James 51, 53
"Peggy Sue" 22–23
Perkins, Carl 1, 4–5, 12, 16, 18, 24, 27, 29, 63–64, 66, 99
Perkins, Jay 63, 66
Perry, Katy 121, 124
Phillips, Sam 29, 62
Pickett, Wilson 68–69
The Platters 120–122
Presley, Elvis 1–7, 9–16, 18–21, 23–24, 29, 33, 37, 40, 42, 51, 53–55, 57–61, 68, 70–71, 75, 78–82, 87, 89, 92–96, 100, 102–105, 107–141
Presley, Priscilla 79–81, 103
Prince (singer) 21, 23

Queen (rock band) 44, 104, 129

Raitt, Bonnie 78, 81
"Rave On" 21–22

RCA Records 2, 92
Richard, Cliff 14, 71
"Ring of Fire" 97–98
Robbins, Marty 54–55
rock and roll 1–2, 24, 30, 33–34, 37, 45–46, 49, 51, 60–61, 80, 94, 129
Rock 'n' Roll Paradise 60, 62
rockabilly 8, 30, 55, 57, 60, 62–63, 65, 67, 73, 76, 91–92, 94, 97, 99
Rockin' E Jamboree 70, 72
Rogers, Johnny 21–23, *22*
The Rolling Stones 3, 42, 44–45, 57, 126
Ross, Diana 2, 73–75
Royal Albert Hall 59, 70
The Royal Hounds 63, 65–67
Royle, Kristy 123–124

St. Angel, Michael 108–110, *108*
"Santa Baby" 42, 44–45
Saucedo, Rick 3, 132
Savoy, Tammi 73–77, *74*
"Separate Ways" 96, 100
The Serendipity Singers 53–55
Shakin' Stevens 14–16, 60
Silver Moon (nightclub) 31–32
Sinatra, Frank 34, 78, 81–82, 96, 116
'68 Comeback Special 8, 12, 14
Slater, Jake 16–18, *17*, 79–80
Slaughter, Cody 5, 20, 76
"So Real" 73, 75
Spider-Man 70, 72
Springsteen, Bruce 87, 108
Stewart, Rod 77, 79, 81
Stone, Ty 67–70, *68*
Storm, Pete 94–96, *95*
Stroud, Luke 29–32, *30*
"Stuck on You" 17–18
Sullivan, Niki 25–26
Sun Records 29, 32, 40, 55, 92, 96
Sun Studio 2, 4–5, 9, 31, 120
Sunset Ballroom 67–68
"Suspicious Minds" 96, 108–109, 112, 115, 117, 124, 126–127, 135, 139–140
Sweetin, Jodie 42, 44–45
"Swipe Right on Me" 97, 99

"Teddy Bear" 10, 12, 131
"That's All Right" 13, 20, 71, 93, 102, 112, 131
That's the Way It Is 96, 136, 138, 141
Thompson, Hank 53, 57, 92
Thompson, Hayden 55–56
Thompson, Johnny 120–125, *121*
Tolliver, Jacob 41–45, *41*
Tony Awards 4, 97, 103
"Travelin' Man" 62, 71
Travelin' Man—The Ricky Nelson Rock 'n' Roll Show 60, 62

151

Index

Trevino, Victor, Jr. 76, 79
A Tribute to the Million Dollar Quartet 111–112
Tubb, Ernest 92–93
Tupelo Elvis Festival 8, 20
"Tutti Frutti" 58–59
Twitty, Conway 21, 29, 86

Ultimate Elvis Tribute Artist Contest 3, 14, 16–17, 94, 102, 111, 113, 115, 125–127, 136–141
"Unchained Melody" 126–127
Underwood, Carrie 121–122, 124

Valens, Ritchie 23, 25, 27
Vance, Willie 92–93
Vavoom Pinups 73, 75

"Waking Up in Vegas" 121, 124
Watkins, Finley 18–20, *19*
Wesley, Elaine 88–90, *89*, 133
Wesley, Garry 88–89, 132–135, *133*

West, Laura 79–81, *80*
Wheels, Bennie 81, 84
"Whole Lotta Shakin' Goin' On" 20, 30–32, 36–38, 42, 45
The Wild One 54, 56
Williams, Hank, Sr. 23, 31, 54, 65, 86, 92
Williams, Larry 37–38
Wilson, Jackie 53, 68–69
Winter Dance Party 23, 25–27
Wonder, Stevie 34, 39, 69
Wood, Darcy Jo 73, 75

Yearwood, Trisha 89, 119
"You Gave Me a Mountain" 126–127, 131, 139
"You Win Again" 36, 40
"You'll Never Walk Alone" 15, 102
"(You're So Square) Baby I Don't Care" 16, 18
"You're the Boss" 79–80

Z, Dean 7, 20, 75, 118, 139, 141

www.ingramcontent.com/pod-product-compliance
Ingram Content Group UK Ltd.
Pitfield, Milton Keynes, MK11 3LW, UK
UKHW042017140426
5217IPUK00015B/1216